SIMPLE WICCA

# SIMPLE

# WICCA

Michele Morgan

CASTLE BOOKS

This edition published in 2002 by Castle Books,
A division of Book Sales Inc.
114 Northfield Avenue, Edison, NJ 08837

Published by arrangement with Conari Press, 2550 Ninth Street, Suite 101,
Berkeley, CA 94710-2551.

   LIBRARY OF CONGRESS CATALOGING-IN-PUBLICATION DATA
Morgan, Michele.
   Simple Wicca / Michele Morgan.
          p.       cm.
  1. Witchcraft.  I. Title.  II.  Series.
  BF1566.M715  2000
  133.4'3—dc21                                          00-029499


Printed in the United States of America.

ISBN: 0-7858-1514-7

*To Mom and Dad ... for believing*

# SIMPLE WICCA

# INTRODUCTION

In truth, there is nothing simple about Wicca. It is a religion, a science, an art, a means of spiritual and self-expression, and a way of life. It is both ancient and contemporary, traditional and ever-changing. There are as many ways to be Wiccan as there are Wiccans; spiritual truths are the sole proprietorship of the individual.

It is my desire, then, in writing this book, to simplify what can seem positively overwhelming by taking you out of the "head" and into the heart of the Wiccan way. If you *experience* something first, it can be far easier to assimilate the myriad details that go into creating it. This book is just that—an experience, offered up in words and images.

The following pages are my invitation to you, to wander a landscape filled with enchantment and wonder . . . seen through my eyes and offered to you simply as a map, in the hopes that you will chart your own course and make your own enchanted discoveries.

*A person travels the world over in search of*
*what he needs, and returns home to find it.*

—George Moore

Blessed be the paths you choose, and wide and varied the way … and may each homecoming prove a priceless gift.

# one

# OUT OF THE BROOM CLOSET: THE WICCAN PHILOSOPHY

*How should we be able to forget those ancient myths, that are at the beginning of all peoples...*

—Rainer Maria Rilke

It is nearly midnight. The "Witching Hour." And tonight there is a full moon. Clouds gather, and skate across the sky; the moon breaks through like a searchlight, huge, so clear you swear you can see the face of childhood nursery rhymes. You pass by the window, and the sudden light bathes you. Something is there, intangible, pulling at you as if the sea suddenly moved in your blood. Something ancient. Irresistible. You find yourself drawn to the door, stepping out into the silver-lit darkness. The wind tangles your hair, pulls at your clothes, smells of woodsmoke and rain and October leaves. You and a sleek gray cat with lantern eyes are the only creatures moving about in this wild darkness.

Having left the house so abruptly, you're without a coat in the autumn chill. Why, then, do you feel as if a fire is burning, somewhere in your rib cage, that your whole body is electric, as bright as the light that pulled you from the safety of your house, drawing you to this spot on the windswept grass?

Somewhere, a clock strikes twelve. You shiver, not from the cold but from a feeling of sacred and timeless connection to the Earth, and to everyone who has ever stood wrapped in a midnight wind, bathed in silver.

Midnight. A full moon. *The Witching Hour*. How can you hear those words and *not* feel something stir inside you? *Witch* is a word that conjures untold images and emotions in even the most steadfast disbeliever; a word that whispers of the ancient and the instinctual; a word charged with mystery.

I have loved the word since I was a child. Despite the common media stereotype of Witches as toad-eating, unbearably ugly, evil old women, I reveled in fantasies of living in a magical cottage by the sea, wearing fabulous flowing dresses, harvesting herbs by moonlight in my stone-walled garden, and stirring up wondrous potions in a cast-iron cauldron.

I was in my late twenties before I began to study what lay behind the fantasies. What I uncovered absolutely validated my imaginings, completely contradicted the stereotypes, and sent me on a spiritual journey that continues to unfold and enrich my life in countless ways.

Wicca, known also as Witchcraft or the Craft of the Wise, is a beautiful and sacred religion, centuries older than Judeo-Christian theosophy. Based on reverence for the Earth and all living creatures, Wicca emphasizes harmony, respect for the rhythms of nature, and the worship of both the male and female aspects of Divinity. At the heart of Wicca is the law "Harm None"; in its soul lies the understanding, expression, and tangible experience of magic.

I was drawn to study the Craft for many reasons. I had always felt different from other people, as though there was an energy turning inside of me that I couldn't name. I felt a kinship with animals, sometimes stronger than that I felt with humans. Storms thrilled me, and moonlight through my bedroom window was rapture. Feathers and stones and chunks of moss *had* to be collected, later to become faerie circles on my windowsill or in my dresser drawer. On summer nights, or when the winter sky was black and sharp as knives, the stars would draw me seemingly out of my skin. And I knew without reason and without a doubt that something truly wonderful was out there waiting for me, if I could just find the way to connect.

Growing up, whenever my family went to church (a sporadic event at best), I remember sitting in the pew and feeling the most tremendous sense of displacement, almost of despair, wondering what in the world was wrong with me. I loved churches themselves, their structure and ambience, the softly glowing windows, the candlelight, the hush of reverence. But as

I got older, the strange sadness grew, and I realized it wasn't that something was wrong—something was *missing*.

Wicca helped me name that something. It wasn't enough for me to sit and listen to someone else tell me about God. I wanted to know God *personally*, to feel and sing and celebrate with Him, to speak *my* words and, most important, to experience the answer.

I began my studies as many modern-day Witches do—I bought a book, took it home, closed the drapes, and moved all the furniture around in my living room so that I could create the semblance of a magical circle. What I lacked in knowledge I more than made up for in enthusiasm—the sheer joy of ritually connecting to Spirit thrilled me to my fingertips.

I wrote and performed rites to celebrate the monthly cycles of the Moon and at Beltane danced around the Maypole (a dowel wedged between the floor and the living-room ceiling, with crepe-paper ribbons . . . but I wore a fabulous flowing dress!). I lit candles to call in the spirits of the four directions, left offerings on my altar to the Celtic goddesses of fire, and earnestly tested the workings of magic. I learned that *Pagan* means "country dweller," not "godless." And, most important, I learned through firsthand experience that Witches aren't evil at all.

*Are you a good Witch, or a bad Witch?*

—Glinda the Good Witch, upon meeting
Dorothy, in the *Wizard of Oz*

It took me quite a while to drum up the courage to "out" myself regarding my spiritual path. Even today, there are times when I am cautious to reveal just what I'm all about. Not because I have a problem with it, but because so many others in the world do—anti-Witchcraft laws were still in effect as late as the middle of the last century! As Marion Weinstein put it in *Positive Magic,* her brilliant book on the occult, "A few years ago I could not have written this book and expected it to be read by the general public. A few hundred years ago, I could not have written this book and expected to live."

In light of the stereotypes and misconceptions surrounding Witches, it's easy to understand the fear, prejudice, and outright hatred sent our way. But I find it incredibly sad how many people in this day and age are so unenlightened, and even sadder still that so many, even when presented with the truth, *choose* to remain unenlightened.

That said, here's what Witches are *not:*

Green. Wart-covered. Able to turn innocent victims into mice, toads, or garden statuary. We do not drink blood, eat small children, nor do we sacrifice *anything* at the crossroads at midnight. We do not take part in any kind of sexual perversion, nor do we seek power through the suffering or oppression of others. We do not put curses or hexes on people, nor do we force, coerce, or magically control anyone against their will. We do not stick pins in dolls, put poison in apples, or raise the dead. We do not have magical "powers"; we can't throw fire from our fingertips, stop time, or conjure objects from thin air. We do not destroy or deface the symbols of other religions, and we do not worship the Devil (more on this, coming up). Most important, we never, ever hurt people, either physically, mentally, spiritually, or magically.

Now, I'm not saying there has never been a Witch who used his or her energies for harmful ends. Just as I'm not saying there has never been a priest who molested young boys, a lawyer or a politician who lied or cheated, or a psychiatrist or doctor who physically or emotionally abused a patient. What I *am* saying is, it is not in the Wiccan faith, practice, or belief system to bring harm to anyone, or anything, *ever.* Period.

So why do the lies persist?

We belong to a culture that thrives on fear, and the original corruption of the pagan faiths, which began as a power play by the medieval Church, has been kept alive and well to a tragic degree ever since.

*There's a little Witch in all of us.*

—Aunt Jett, in the movie *Practical Magic*

## WHAT IS A WITCH?

Witches, for the most part, are fairly ordinary people; generally speaking, you can't tell a Witch simply by appearances.

What sets Witches apart, however, is how they live their lives. Wicca teaches you to look at the world through magical eyes, to see the fabulous in the mundane, to care for and tend your days with consciousness. At the root of *Wicca* is the word *wic,* meaning "to bend" or "shape." Witches bend and shape the innate laws and energies of nature through ritual, prayer, and spellcasting, to produce positive ends in the physical world. This is the essence of magic, and magic is the lifeblood of the Craft.

In *Wicca: A Guide for the Solitary Practitioner,* Scott Cunningham defines magic as "the projection of natural energies to produce needed results." Magic is the focused use of language, will, action, and emotion, and the shifting of consciousness to achieve spiritual communion.

All religions practice magic in some form, through the rites and ceremonies performed by their priests. Wicca embraces magic as a spiritual practice for *everyone,* and Witches work with magic consciously and deliberately. Prayer is a form of magic. Chanting, singing, dancing, affirmations, meditation, visualization—all are magical in nature. A ritual or spell is merely a corporeal prayer, the magical aspects of which are made all the more powerful by the physical interpretation.

Witches use magic as a way to communicate with Spirit, to consecrate our ritual space, and to better ourselves and the world around us. Wiccan magic is natural and harmonious, a sacred and wondrous aspect of our faith.

The word *religion* means to "re-link," or "bind back." As a Pagan, or nature, religion, Wicca links us to the original concepts of deity by our earliest ancestors, the idea that God or Spirit resides in all things, and within each of us as spiritual beings. In Wicca, there is no separation between human and Spirit. Rather than some far-off, unreachable, omnipotent being, God is manifest in a hundred miraculous ways, in the day-to-day rituals of life as well as in the larger, more mystical patterns of the universe.

Wicca sees the Earth as a living Goddess, who blesses us and must be nurtured and cared for in return. Wiccans honor and work with the cycles of nature and the seasons rather than trying to dominate their environment. The Wheel of the Year, the Wiccan sacred calendar, is marked by eight festivals that celebrate the eternal circle of life, as witnessed in nature by the changing of the seasons and the natural cycles of birth, maturation, death, and resurrection.

Because of this deep connection to the Earth and her mysteries, natural lifestyle choices are common among Witches. Ecological issues are of great importance, as are social issues such as equality of the sexes and racial diversity. The feminist movement in the late 1960s had a great deal to do with the resurgence of the Craft and the Goddess religions, bringing a much-needed counterbalance to the patriarchal systems that have dominated Western culture for centuries. Though still bucking the tide in some regards, Wicca continues to make significant marks in the areas of personal and global responsibility, environmental action, and multicultural relations.

Wicca is a highly individualistic and experiential faith, with a strong ethical code based on moral and personal responsibility. There is no "confession" or absolution of sins by an outside authority; instead, Wiccans are required to face up to their actions, admit their mistakes, and set things right whenever they can. Wiccans also believe in reincarnation, which deepens their commitment to personal and spiritual growth, and to learning from all experiences.

Another aspect that differentiates a Witch is the practice of intuitive and psychic abilities. In the Craft, you learn to work with all the senses, and to become especially attuned to your instinctual voice through the use of divinatory tools. Many Witches focus on specific methods of meditation and achieving altered states of consciousness in their ritual and magical workings. Tarot cards, pendulums, crystals, and runes are tools commonly used by Witches to access the realms of psychic perception.

Unlike organized Judeo-Christian religions, Wicca adheres to very few set precepts or doctrines. Rather, there are certain beliefs held sacred by all Wiccans, from which the individual Craft traditions and practices spring. This lack of absolutes by no means indicates a lack of conviction; because Wicca's system of ethics comes from personal honor rather than imposed dogma, Wiccans are highly committed to "walking their talk" in all aspects of their lives.

Three principles serve as the foundation for the Wiccan way of life:

**The Wiccan Rede:** *"An ye harm none, do as ye will."* In essence, this rule says do whatever you like, as long as it doesn't bring harm to yourself or to another. This is *not* an invitation to run amuck without repercussion. This principal requires a high degree of consciousness in terms of assessing the myriad physical, emotional, mental, and spiritual consequences related to any particular action. In other words, this tenet says "Look well before you leap, and make darn sure you're not going to land on anybody else."

**The Threefold Law:** *"What you do comes back to you three-fold."* Another principle of consequence, the Threefold Law is like the Buddhist notion of karma, pointing out the inevitable return of expended energy. This relates to physical action as well as emotional thought forms; kindness extended comes back magnified, as does negativity and ill will. This principle in particular governs the magic that Wiccans practice; no true Witch would ever put a curse on someone, or even consider performing "black magic," lest it come back to them three times worse!

**The Golden Rule:** *"Do unto others as you would have them do unto you."* This is pretty self-explanatory and, as with the other two principles, puts responsibility for right action straight in the lap of the individual. The Golden Rule creates an environment of respect for everyone; most Wiccans have dealt with prejudice of one sort or another from the outside world, and so tend to be even more accepting of anyone or anything "different."

One of the most fascinating aspects of the Craft is its autonomous, eclectic approach to worship, encouraging followers to develop a personal religious practice, gleaned from one's own experiences, wisdom, and instincts. A sense of spiritual diversity is key to the Craft, as Wicca is polytheistic (meaning "believing in more than one God") in nature.

I've always said that God doesn't care what you call Him, as long as you call Him. Wicca gives you myriad names with which to connect to Spirit. The Gods and Goddesses worshiped in the Craft are as diverse as the people who choose them: the Sun King, the Green Man, Herne, the Lord of the Hunt, and the Triple Goddess of the Moon, who is Maiden, Mother, and Crone. There are also the Greek, Celtic, Norse, and Egyptian deities, and many more. Each is fascinating, mythic. Each has a specific energy and personality. In Wicca, who you worship and how you worship is a personal, sacred choice, which makes for a truly intimate bond between human and Spirit.

Wiccans respect the idea that different spiritual beliefs work for different people. In fact, many Witches add aspects of other religious systems, such as Native American Shamanism or Buddhism, to their rituals and practices. Others work closely with Catholic saints, angels, and Jesus Christ. Religion is the language of spirituality, and Wiccans are definitely multilingual!

> *Witchcraft is comforting. You learn that the night is as beautiful as the daytime, that the dark and the light are equal, that neither is better than the other... that life and death exist beside one another, as a balance.*

> —Reverend Judith Laxer, Priestess of the Goddess, LunaSea coven

Another distinguishing factor of the Wiccan path is the acknowledgment, and even celebration, of Darkness. (Here's where the misinformed really go to town espousing the "evils" of Witchcraft!) Let me set the record straight. Darkness, in the Craft, is *not* the Devil or Satan or anything evil. It is night, death, the dark of the Moon before She comes round to new again; the understanding that for every creation there is an inevitable cycle of entropy. Wicca is nature based and, just as in nature, when plants die, compost down into the Earth, and serve to nourish new growth, the Darkness honored in Wicca is a natural part of life.

Indeed, not only do Witches *not* worship the Devil, Witches don't even believe in the Devil! Because of the Craft's tenets regarding personal responsibility and morality, the concept of an Absolute Evil doesn't hold any water with Witches. Besides,

Satan is a Christian fallen angel, not a Pagan god, and while some Witches may adopt certain aspects of other religions, Old Scratch is definitely not a candidate.

In a culture that fears and attempts to deny death, Wicca stands out as a path that honors it as part of the cycle of life. Wiccans see death as a transition, a journeying on to the next plane of existence, knowing the soul will be reborn in whatever form it chooses.

Finally, Wicca is *fun!* The joyful, celebratory nature of the Craft invites the child in all of us to come out and play, to meet Spirit with a sense of innocence and wonder. And the act of performing magic is pure enchantment. Think childhood treasure hunts, games of make-believe and storytelling; fairy dust and bubbles, candlelight, ribbons and wishes, and lavender ink on handmade paper. Of course, there is also a serious side to magic, and to the Craft—concentration, intent, energy projection. But even in the serious moments, Wicca incites the imagination, engages the soul, and helps you put your energies into creative, tangible focus. How can that not be fun?

> *Bide within the Law you must,*
> *in perfect Love and perfect Trust.*
> *Live you must and let to live,*
> *fairly take and fairly give...*
>
> —The Wiccan Rede

Unfortunately, no talk of Witches would be complete without touching upon the particular history of the Craft known as the Burning Times.

The persecution of Witches is legendary. With the advent of early Christianity and its monotheistic system, the Pagan religions of Europe became immediately suspect to the doctrines of the Church. Conversion was Christianity's first attempt at religious monopoly; the Pagan festivals were replaced under Church directive with Christian holy days, and Christian temples were erected on ancient sites of Pagan worship.

Pagans went underground, continuing to observe their rites and customs in secret, and, for a time, Christianity and the Old Religion existed side-by-side, somewhat peaceably. However, by the end of the thirteenth century, edicts had been passed proclaiming witchcraft, and anyone practicing it, evil. The most infamous of these was the *Malleus malificarum*, or *The Witches' Hammer*, a manual for Witch-hunters published in 1486 by Heinrich Kraemer and Jacob Sprenger, which gave detailed instructions for identifying, torturing, and putting to death anyone who met the "criteria" for a Witch. (Ironically, most of those being killed weren't actually Witches, and most of those doing the killing weren't actual clerics.)

The old Pagan gods became the Devils of the "new" religion; fear and collective hysteria fed the fires. Exposing a Witch was considered a moral and spiritual victory, and as land became a commodity to be bought and sold, it became even bigger business to turn in friends, neighbors, even family members!

The campaign against Witches reached critical mass in the late fifteenth century. It has been estimated that anywhere from half a million to 13 million men, women, and children (with a predominance of women) were tortured and put to death by the end of the seventeenth century. This dark and brutal period of history remains a terrifying tribute to greed, misconception, political manipulation, and religious intolerance.

The fallacies continue to this day. My copy of Merriam-Webster's Collegiate Dictionary (revised edition, copyright 1978) defines Witch as "one that is credited with malignant supernatural powers; a woman practicing black witchcraft often with the aid of a devil or familiar; an ugly old woman."

Just last fall at a local farmers' market, I picked up a leaflet published by a Christian organization warning parents about Halloween, and the spiritual, moral, and physical dangers to their children from "Satanists and Witches."

From Snow White to Samantha Stevens and Sabrina the Teenage Witch, modern-day Witches have been consistently portrayed as either meddlers in dark magic, utterly evil, or, at the very least, nose-wiggling, bumbling, but lovable fools.

Witches are none of those things. They are healers, teachers, mystics, and poets; stewards of the Earth, and lovers of life and balance. And they are keepers of the Old Ways, guardians of a wisdom that is ancient and profound, from a time when the world was new and Man and God walked the Earth together.

As you journey through the pages of this little book, it is my hope that you will find truth to feed your spiritual yearnings, magic to feed your soul, and light to scatter the shadows that have darkened the Wiccan path for so many centuries.

# two

# YESTERDAY, TODAY:
# THE TRADITIONS OF WITCHCRAFT

*So what is truth today, may tomorrow only*
*partially be so to a developing soul.*

—Edgar Cayce

In the years since its modern revival, Wicca has grown much like a wise woman's garden—neatly lain and bordered beds, the landscape having a certain ordered pattern, yet within the structure a constantly unfolding surprise of color and perfume. There is always room for the odd wildflower among the lilies; a seed, carried on the wind or the wing of a bird, is certain to pop up as a daisy or marigold in the middle of the sage. The very nature of Wicca creates fertile ground for all manner of Craft Traditions to flourish.

A "Tradition" in Wicca is a specific practice or way of worshiping the God and Goddess, handed down, Witch to Witch, over time. Traditions are primarily the structure of a *coven,* a group of Wiccans who come together to form a community and to participate in group rituals and magic-working. Although the Traditions practiced today are relatively young compared to Wicca's pre-Christian Pagan roots, they are based upon the Old Ways.

It is impossible to know the authentic practices of the Craft that existed before the Burning Times, as few Pagans of that era knew how to write, and much of the Craft knowledge died with those who carried it. Today's Traditions are woven from the secrets that managed to survive, legends passed down through the ages, and the instinctual, sacred connection to Earth and Spirit shared by all humankind.

Through the years, certain Traditions have changed, while others have stayed true. Some covens choose to follow a specific Tradition closely; others combine and experiment as they journey along the path. Even within the individual Traditions, there are "wildflowers"—sects of Witches who find spiritual inspiration in literature or myth, and add their particular colors to the already established order.

## THE TRADITIONS

Following are a few of the better-known Traditions followed by today's Witches, (in alphabetical order) with brief descriptions of their practices, to give you a basic layout of the "garden":

**Alexandrian:** Founded in the 1960s by Alex Sanders, this Tradition is said to be a modified version of the Gardnerian system, though a bit less stringent. There is a more eclectic approach to ritual, with a blending of cabalistic teachings and ceremonial magic.

**British Traditional:** Adhering to a mix of Gardnerian and Celtic Traditions, coven members train through a structured degree system, and follow the studies of Janet and Stewart Farrar. Other Traditional or Traditionalist systems are based on the customs, myths, and literature of a particular geographic area, such as Welsh, Scottish, and Irish. Again, these tend to be structured in their practices and not particularly open to new members.

**Celtic:** This Tradition has the distinct feel of the Druids (an ancient Celtic priesthood), with a strong focus on the Earth, the elements, and tree magic. Runes are a significant tool for the Celtic Witch, and the deities worshiped are primarily of Celtic origin.

**Dianic:** This Western European Tradition can be traced back to Margaret Murray in 1921. A mixture of many Traditions, its primary focus is worship of the Goddess, in particular the Goddess Diana. In certain instances, Dianic Traditions have completely excluded the male aspect of Divinity, leading Dianic Wicca to be tagged the "feminist" movement of the Craft.

**Eclectic:** The most modern of the Traditions, which is basically nontraditional! The Eclectic Wiccan will mix and match different Traditions, using what suits him or her best. This is perhaps the most popular form of Wicca, particularly among solitary practitioners, as it allows for complete freedom within the framework of the Craft.

**Faerie:** A Tradition based on faerie lore, combining Celtic and Druidic systems with elemental and "green," or natural, magic.

**Gardnerian:** Founded by Gerald Gardner in Great Britain in the 1950s, this Tradition claims to have survived in secret since the Burning Times. Gardner achieved notoriety and earned the title "Official Witch of Britain" as one of the first Witches to go public with his book, *Witchcraft Today,* published in 1954. Today, the Gardnerian Tradition continues to adhere to very structured practices, including a hierarchical grading system, ritual nudity, and secretive initiations of new members.

**Hereditary:** This Tradition is based on family lineage. A Hereditary Witch can trace the Craft generations back on their family tree, and has been taught their practice by a living relative. Most Hereditary Traditions are quite secretive, and are closed to anyone outside of the family; some teach only one or two people in each generation. Though very rare, a Hereditary Tradition will sometimes adopt outsiders into their practice, usually due to a dwindling family line.

**Kitchen Witch:** One whose practice is centered mainly around hearth and home, focusing on the practical side of Earth and elemental magic and religion. This Tradition is popular among suburban and city Wiccans, emphasizing magic in domestic and work environments.

**Pictish:** A Scottish Tradition with a strong connection to nature and the animal, vegetable, and mineral kingdoms, this solitary form of the Craft focuses primarily on magic, with little religious content.

**Seax-Wica:** Also known as Saxon-Wica, this Tradition was founded by Raymond Buckland in 1973 as an alternative to the existing Gardnerian and Alexandrian practices. This Tradition allows for solitary practitioners and self-initiation, and served to relax the strictures regarding creation of new covens.

**Strega:** A Tradition started in Italy around 1353, this is considered one of the oldest unchanged forms of Witchcraft, and the teachings are profound and quite lyrical.

**Teutonic/Nordic:** This ancient Tradition is rooted in the agricultural and warrior tribes of Scandinavia and northern Germany, with an emphasis on Nordic culture. The deities most commonly worshiped are the Goddess Freya and the God Odin.

So how do you decide upon a Tradition? First, do some studying. Get in touch with your local Craft community, or hop on the Internet and ask questions. Then ask *yourself* some questions. Does a certain mythic era appeal to you? Do you feel drawn to an older, more established system, or do you envision creating your own rituals, making it all up as you go along?

Most important, you must trust your instincts, and allow your passion wings. Wicca is a multifaceted, unorthodox spiritual adventure; there is a great deal of freedom in any given practice. Find the path (or paths!) that calls to you, that stirs your imagination and makes you feel as though you've come home.

## COVENS

*One to call the circle, two to fan the fire,*
*Ten to raise the cone of power*
*to the heavens higher.*
*Thirteen standing in a round,*
*strike the drum a joyful beat,*
*Call the Goddess Moon come down,*
*Merry in our circle Meet.*

—Coven song

A coven usually numbers no more than thirteen, the number thirteen having ancient symbolic roots in the Craft, as it represents the thirteen moons in every calendar year. Covens can be comprised of both men and women, although some covens limit themselves to same-sex membership as a matter of preference or Tradition.

At the spiritual helm of the coven is the Priestess, who leads the rites and stands as representative of the Goddess. With the aplomb of an actress, the tenderness of a mother, and the grace of a diplomat in counsel, she supports and nurtures the coven and its members, guides them in their personal growth, and offers spiritual and magical advice to new initiates. The Priestess will often choose a Priest, who is responsible for the administrative and organizational aspects of the coven, and whom represents the God in ritual workings. The other members of the coven are by no means simple observers; everyone has an opportunity to participate, conduct, and have input into the ceremonies of the group. Some covens forgo the hierarchy of appointed leaders altogether, choosing instead to interchange duties among the members, giving everyone equal opportunity to explore the Priest or Priestess within.

Covens generally gather for the eight Craft festivals marking the Wheel of the Year and twice in the month for the new and full moons. Then, depending on the individual coven and its customs, they might meet during the waxing moon for spellcasting, the waning moon for banishing rituals, or at any other time magic is needed or desired. Some covens meet once a week as a matter of course, to keep the creative and cooperative energies flowing. A coven is much like a large, close-knit family; the personalities and passions of the individual members combining to create a living, alchemical organism.

Seeking a coven is a magical quest. Since Wicca is not a

religion that strives to convert others to its beliefs, most covens find that their members are drawn to them when the time is right and the spiritual need presents itself. Be assured that if you are serious in your pursuit of the Wiccan path, doorways will open and serendipitous meetings will happen. Through studying books, taking classes, and contact with the local Craft community, you will find like-minded groups or individuals to connect with. As it is said, "When the student is ready, the teacher appears."

## THE SOLITARY PATH

*When all is said and done I think every Witch should, at some time, face the moon alone, feet planted on the ground, with only his or her voice chanting in the starry night.*

—Laurie Cabot, *Power of the Witch*

Not every Witch need seek out a coven. Solitaries are individuals who prefer to practice the Craft on their own, working their rituals privately and pacing their spiritual journey as they see fit. As Wicca continues to evolve, more practitioners are choosing the Solitary path over that of the coven. While Solitaries may lack the support and group energy of a coven, they obviously have greater freedom in terms of adapting rituals to suit their individual needs, and in the ability to work magic quickly and quietly, in any situation.

For a Solitary, initiation into the Craft and dedication to the God and Goddess are usually self-conducted. Some Solitaries practice magic and moon rituals on their own, then choose to celebrate the Craft holidays with other Solitaries or covens in order to experience the beauty and power of group ritual.

# three

# HEAVEN, EARTH, AND THE POWERS THAT BE: THE GODS AND GODDESSES OF WICCA

*The best form is to worship God in every form.*

—Neem Karoli Baba

Nowhere else is Wicca's diverse and eclectic nature made more apparent than in the freedom to choose whom you worship. For most people, this concept of choice regarding God is nearly impossible to comprehend. At the same time, choosing a deity is part of what makes Wicca so appealing to those who have become dissatisfied with mainstream religious structures.

So what is the point of choosing? Of naming God anything other than God?

As human beings, we define ourselves by what fits us. Things work, or they don't. We like, or we dislike; we adore, or we hate. We identify with, empathize with, relate to, understand . . . or we don't have a clue. Naming God is about choosing what works for you, spiritually; what you like, love, identify with, *relate to,* in order to define who you are in spiritual relationship.

Silver RavenWolf, in her book *To Ride a Silver Broomstick,* compares the idea of Wiccan deities to a family tree, with "the All," or universal energy, at the top. The Lord and the Lady are next in line, representing the perfectly balanced male and female aspects of Divinity paramount to the Wiccan belief system. And last, closest to where we humans stand on terra firma, are the Gods and Goddesses in all their rich and varied guises.

I see the Gods and Goddesses of Wicca much like the subpersonalities of the human psyche. They are different aspects, or different temperaments, if you will, of the All. And just as you would choose a friend based on similarities in energy or traits you were drawn to instinctively or emotionally, so too you can choose your favorite representation of Spirit with which to create a working partnership.

*The Awakening has begun!*

—William Dempsey

When I first "picked up the broomstick," as we say in Wicca, all the different choices rather overwhelmed me. I'm a double Sagittarian—I don't like researching, I like doing. I didn't want to have to learn all the Gods and Goddesses and then figure out who I wanted to invoke in my rituals. I wanted to get right down to business!

Of course, one of the best things about all the choices in the Craft is that you can also choose not to choose. So I began my Wiccan experience quite simply, with only the God and the Goddess, or, as I called them, the Lord and Lady of Magic. I still invoke them today, both in ritual and prayer, and think of them as liaisons of Spirit, my confidants in all things magical.

The idea of twin deities is one of the oldest aspects of Wicca, based on the principles of duality and reverence for the male and female energies inherent in nature. There are many ways to see the God and Goddess. From ancient times, they have been known as the Horned God, Lord of the Hunt, and the Triple Goddess, who is linked to the three phases of the Moon.

The God represents the Sun. He is born at the Winter Solstice, and his power grows through the year until Midsummer, when he reaches the zenith of his days; then he wanes in accordance with the shortening daylight hours, and ultimately "dies," only to be born again on the longest night of the year. The God can also be seen as that which is physical in nature— the tangible world, physical strength, sexual passion, the harvest, and the hunt. He is sometimes referred to as the consort of the Goddess, which in no way makes him lesser than she.

The Goddess is known as the Universal Mother, the Creatrix, the keeper of the eternal cycle of life, death, and life renewed. But she can also be seen as the ethereal world—reason, intuition, logic, and dreams. The Triple Goddess is comprised of three faces, for the waxing, full, and waning Moons.

She is at once the Maiden, who is the sweet innocence of youth; the Mother, who represents fertility and nurturing; and the Crone, who is wisdom and, ultimately, death.

Together, the God and Goddess are exquisitely balanced in energy, like shadow and flame, each the other's perfect complement, neither greater nor more deserving of worship than the other. Like the Chinese symbol of *yin* (earth) and *yang* (heaven), the feminine and masculine aspects of Spirit coexist within all things, and cannot exist one without the other. They are also seen as archetypes from the Tarot deck—the Magician and the High Priestess, or the Emperor and the Empress, respectively. Partners.

The beauty of the Wiccan path lies in the freedom to create your own personal experience of worship. No doctrine dictates who or what the God and Goddess must be; rather, there are ancient and symbolic descriptions of their energies, and essences. The rest is, happily, up to you. Do you desire a God who is tough or tender? Do you picture him bronze-skinned or fair? Is your Goddess slender, or plump like the fruit swelling on the vine, with hair as golden as the September wheatfields?

The only rule, as stated in the Wiccan Rede, is "in perfect Love and perfect Trust." The God and Goddess are not pious, vengeful, judgmental, or cruel. They are Divine Love, incarnate, and whatever physical form you choose to give them is creativity at its highest.

I envision the Lord as strong, handsome, with dark hair and

electric eyes. He is protective and passionate, the master of manifestation, who holds the energies of the universe in his hands. He wears a headdress made from the horns of a stag, and a robe embroidered with an image of the Sun, stitched with threads of real gold. He stands at my right, the placement of the masculine force, and represents the forests, the fields, the mountains, the desert plains, and the beasts that roam those landscapes.

The Lady is hauntingly beautiful, with flowing black hair that reflects the light of the full Moon as it dances above her. She is the essence of the Mother, a wise and instinctual creature who births, rears, then lovingly releases her offspring into the world, armed with knowledge and magic. She wears a blue silk robe, the color of the sea after a storm, and holds a crystal ball in one hand, a book of ancient secrets in the other. She stands at my left, for the feminine, and represents Earth, ocean, and sky. The winged and the water creatures are just some of her varied companions, and a pentacle, the symbol of the Craft, hangs from a silver chain just above her heart.

I imbued my God and Goddess with the characteristics and energies I desired, traits that fulfilled and satisfied my imaginings, and made me love them, fiercely. I walk in the world with them and feel comforted and safe; they give me strength, courage, and the fire to fuel my passions.

> *From the Creative and the Receptive emerge the*
> *ten thousand things.*
>
> —Chinese proverb

As I continued on the Wiccan path, I soon ventured to explore some of the other Gods and Goddesses, and quickly found out how powerful it was to call on and work with their energies. Each of the Gods and Goddesses belongs to a specific *pantheon,* or group of deities serving a particular culture or people. I was immediately drawn to the Celtic pantheon, based in part upon my heritage (Welsh, on my mother's side), and the fact that anything medieval or Arthurian in legend thrills me to my bones. But I also connected to some from the Egyptian and Greek mythologies, and found that each had a distinct and definite flavor.

The deities in Wicca aren't jealous or possessive, and don't mind sharing the spotlight, or candlelight, as the case may be. So my rituals began to include one or two of the mythical Goddesses, as well as my beloved Lord and Lady; rather like guest stars appearing on a favorite TV show.

Wicca allows you to develop a constant, interactive relationship with Spirit in as simple a way as seeing the Moon come up through the trees and feeling a breathless kinship to Her beauty and power, to receiving specific assistance for anything from finding a parking space to mending a relationship.

Hestia, the Greek Goddess of home and hearth, once led me serendipitously to a wonderful little house in the city for half the rent I was expecting to pay, even managing to include a claw-foot bathtub I had asked for at the last minute on a whim. And Bast, an Egyptian Goddess of protection who comes in the form of a giant black panther, has not only walked me unscathed many times through disorderly crowds and down dark streets, but has kept my last two cars purring like kittens well into their prime. (The first car stayed on the road about seventy thousand miles beyond its life expectancy, and during a tune-up, the mechanic asked, jokingly, "What did you do, put a spell on this car or something?" I just smiled.)

There is no denying the power of these ancient energies. Because the deities each have their own individual mythos and symbolism, they can be invoked for precise needs, rather like choosing a medical specialist over a general practitioner to treat an illness. And the number of deities is staggering—one source I found on the Internet claims to list seventeen hundred!

Choosing your patron Gods or Goddesses is similar to finding a Tradition—gather all the information you can and, most important, *listen to your instincts*. A particular pantheon or deity may not appeal to you as much as others. Trust what you're drawn to. As your spiritual muscles develop and strengthen, you'll want to stretch them; venture into different pantheons and look around.

One word of caution, however, particularly when you're first learning the Craft: Don't take the deities lightly. They are powerful, tangible, and should absolutely be respected. As with any personality, some have a sharper side to them and need to be worked with carefully. Take the time to learn about whichever God or Goddess entreats your attention. The path of Wicca requires tremendous consciousness and integrity; traits that, well developed, will serve you not only in the Craft but in every aspect of your life.

Following is a brief list of some of the more commonly known Gods and Goddesses of Wicca; a sampling of names and their corresponding energies, which will give you but a taste of the possibilities.

## THE GODDESSES

**Aphrodite:** The Greek Goddess of passion, erotic love, beauty, and the feminine force, she symbolizes feminine prowess, sensuality, sexuality, relationship, and flower magic. Call on Aphrodite when you want to spice up your intimate partnership, or when you're in need of connecting to your own inner beauty and feminine soul.

**Aradia:** An Italian Goddess known as "Queen of the Witches." in legend, Aradia came to Earth to teach her mother Diana's magic to mortals. She symbolizes the Moon and the element of air. Invoke her protection and guidance on your Wiccan path, and for any Moon magic or ritual.

**Athena:** A Greek Goddess of war and wisdom, Athena's dual nature, of both storms and peace, battle and education, gives her a reputation as a warrior and a protectress. Call on her if you're experiencing challenges on the work front or in school, particularly those involving conflict with others.

**Bast:** An Egyptian Goddess of protection, Bast is also known as Bastet and symbolizes cats, healing, childbirth, pleasure, passion, joy, and the element of fire. Besides being a resourceful traveling companion, she can be counted on to watch over your own four-leggeds (particularly those of the feline persuasion), your car, and your physical body, and she can greatly aid women in labor. One of my favorite deities, Bast has a penchant for showing up in tangible and intriguing ways.

**Brigid:** One of the Triple Goddesses of the Celtic pantheon, she was so loved in Ireland that she was made a saint by the Catholic Church. She represents both the elements of fire and water, the Heavenly Mother, and creative inspiration, and is a powerful protectress, especially of children. Invoke her for any creative endeavor, issues of fertility, assistance in childbirth, blessing and purification of a well or water source, and the guardianship of children and animals.

**Demeter:** An Earth Mother Goddess of the Greek pantheon, in legend Demeter was the mother of Persephone, a maiden who was abducted by Hades and taken to the Underworld, where she lives for six months of every year, thus bringing death and winter to the world. Demeter is a powerful Goddess to call on in childbirth, as well as for the protection of small children.

**Diana:** A Roman Moon Goddess and mother figure for Witches, Diana represents luck, the hunt, the power of the Moon, and general magic. Ask for her energy in any magical working. She is of particular assistance when you are searching for something, either within yourself or without; or when you need intuitive "light" shed on a certain situation.

**Hecate:** Known as the Goddess of the Dark Moon, she is the Crone in Greek mythology. Hecate symbolizes blessing and banishing, endings and beginnings, luck, divination, the Moon in its waning or dark phase, oracles, prophecy, women's mysteries, and death. Hecate is present in any rite of passage, whether it be the release of a relationship, a behavior pattern or belief system that is no longer desired, or the crossing over of a soul from this life to the next. Call on her in any spell or situation that requires letting go and the wisdom and the power of the feminine sage.

**Hera:** A Greek Goddess of matrimony and the cycles of women's growth, in legend she was married to the God Zeus, and became quite jealous of his affairs with mortal women. Hera represents love, the Moon, motherhood, and the element of air. Invoke her during rites of handfasting, marriage, or commitment; just be aware of the envious or vindictive aspects of her nature. She will keep you honest in love.

**Hestia:** Another of the Greek Goddesses, Hestia rules the home and hearth. She symbolizes fire, domestic and kitchen magic, conception, and the safety and well-being of self and family. The perfect Goddess to attend a house blessing, help with finding, purchasing, or renovating a home, spring-cleaning rituals, or protection for children home alone after school. She is also a wonderful companion for babysitters!

**Kali:** A Hindu Goddess of creation and destruction, Kali represents protection, divination, creation, and combat. She is a particular guardian of abused women and children. If a woman is in fear of physical danger or attack, Kali's name can be invoked with awesome results.

**Persephone:** The Greek Goddess of the Underworld, spring, and the harvest. In legend, she is the daughter of Demeter, and is celebrated at the Spring Equinox, when she returns from the Underworld bringing life back to the Earth. She represents love, maidenhood, and the element of earth. Invite her into your garden, the beginning of a relationship or a business venture, and call on her knowledge of the duality of light and dark that balances all things.

**Selene:** A Greek Moon Goddess symbolic of solutions, logic, and women's rights. In legend, she was a teacher to magicians and sorcerers. She is seen as the full Moon, illuminating all. Invoke her during full Moon rituals, when you seek a logical answer to a question or problem, or in any situation involving equality and fairness for women.

**Adonis:** He is the partner of Aphrodite. A Greek God of plants and flowers, he symbolizes love, fertility, health, and the element of earth. Ask for his help with gardens, exercise and diet, recuperation from illness, preventative medicine, and the physical aspects of love.

**Apollo:** A Greek God of the Sun, light, music, and the arts. He is the twin of Artemis, a Greek Moon Goddess. Apollo can help you connect with your creative muse, free the artist that hides within your logical mind, and can assist in healing depression, especially from Seasonal Affective Disorder.

**Cernunnos:** The Celtic Horned God, also known as Herne the Hunter, and the most commonly worshiped God-form in Wicca. Cernunnos, along with the God Pan, became the paradigm for Christianity's Satan, as a device for destroying the Old Religions in Europe. Cernunnos represents the hunt, the woodlands, male fertility, magic, and animals. Call on him when you are in need of strong male protection, luck in conception, or in any ecological or environmental issue, particularly involving timber, old-growth forests, and endangered species.

**Eros:** A Greek God of romance and love and the son of the Goddess Aphrodite, Eros is also associated with the Roman God Cupid. He represents all things romantic, poetic, and sensual in love. Ask for his help with intimacy issues, to fan the flame of desire in relationship, or to connect to your own passionate, erotic nature.

**Ganesha:** A God of India who represents good fortune, literature, and wisdom, he appears with the head of an elephant and the body of a man. Call on Ganesha to ensure success and financial gain in any new business venture, in any magical working regarding money or wealth, to support your reputation, and to garner the respect of others.

**Horus:** The God of the "all-seeing eye" in the Egyptian pantheon, the son of Isis and Osiris is a God of light and healing who appears with the head of a falcon and the body of a man. Invoke his powerful energy during a health crisis to aid in diagnosis, treatment, and recovery, or in any situation where enlightenment is needed.

**Lugh:** This Celtic God of the Sun, light, and the harvest, whose name literally means "The Shining One," is celebrated each year at Lughnasadh, the Pagan festival of the harvest in August. Lugh is a warrior God who represents strength, power, youth, and victory. Connect with him for business ventures, money issues, and for protection.

**Mithra:** A Persian Sun God and bringer of light, Mithra is considered a soldier's God who guides and protects the warrior in battle. He is associated with the mystery of magic, fertility, and the element of air. Ask for his help in any situation that requires strength, perseverance, courage, and magical assistance.

**Odin:** A warrior's God in the Norse pantheon, Odin carries the energy of wisdom, magic, war, and the Underworld. He is also representative of poetry, creativity, divination, prophecy, and luck. Call on Odin to imbue you with the heart of a warrior and a poet's soul.

**Osiris:** An Egyptian God of life and death, in legend he was the husband of Isis and the father of Horus. He represents fertility, growing things, the afterlife, intellect, charm, and balance. Invoke his energy for connecting to the cycles of nature, for help in accepting the passing of a loved one, for welcoming change, and when making important decisions.

**Pan:** A Greek God of the woodlands and fertility, whose Celtic alter ego is Cernunnos. Like him, Pan was demonized by the Christian church for his embodiment of lust, fertility, and unabashed eroticism. Pan is associated with the element of earth, and can be called upon in matters concerning sexual performance, potency, libido, and infusing a run-of-the-mill love life with freedom and playfulness.

**Taleisin:** A Welsh God who is a poet and a harper, Taleisin is associated with sages, seers, wizards, and initiates in the occult arts. It is said that he lives in the domain of the summer stars.

Seek his energy in any aspect of creativity, particularly music and writing, and in the study of magic.

**Thor:** The Norse God of thunder and the sky, Thor is known as a peasant's God, defender of the working class. In legend, the sound of thunder is his chariot rolling across the sky. Thor symbolizes protection, defense, law and order, and justice. Ask for his assistance in situations that demand authority, the constructive release of anger, and when you're having difficulty expressing emotions.

> *The beginning of wisdom is to call things by their right names.*
>
> —Chinese proverb

So many deities, so little time.... Take your time. There is no hurry to become an expert on the pantheons. Start slowly, with deliberation, to learn about the Gods and Goddesses that speak to you. As Janet and Stewart Farrar wrote in *The Witches' Bible*, "Thoughtful consideration before the choice is in itself a magical act."

# four

# A YEAR IN THE LIFE: THE WICCAN DAYS OF CELEBRATION

*Ye who love the haunts of nature ... listen to
these wild traditions....*

—Henry Wadsworth Longfellow,
"The Song of Hiawatha"

The foundation of the Wiccan faith is the celebration of Spirit in nature. And Wicca is nothing if not a celebratory religion. The path of the Sun, the phases of the Moon, the first crocus pressing through February snow—all are magical grounds for ceremony in the Craft.

In ancient times, our ancestors lived in harmony with the Earth. Mother Nature and her rhythms were not only understood and worked with, they were honored and exalted. From these earliest observances of seasons and cycles come the Days of Power, the sacred holidays that comprise the Wiccan calendar, or, as it is known in the Craft, the Wheel of the Year. The image of an ever-turning wheel is symbolic of the Wiccan view of life; the constancy of change, the flow of season into season, and humankind's inseparable relationship with the Earth.

The "spokes" of the Wheel are the *Sabbats,* or solar holidays, which consecrate the Sun's yearly journey across the skies. There are eight Sabbats, which divide the year by natural events. Four of the Sabbats, known as the *quarters,* mark the astronomical beginnings of the seasons: Yule, or the Winter Solstice (circa December 21); Ostara, or the Spring Equinox (circa March 21); Midsummer, or the Summer Solstice (circa June 21); and Mabon, or the Fall Equinox (circa September 21).

The remaining four Sabbats are called the *cross quarters.* These holidays are based in part upon old agricultural festivals such as the birthing of the first lambs (Imbolc, February 2), the fertility of the growing fields (Beltane, May 1), the time of the harvest (Lughnasadh, August 1), and the sacrifice of animals for winter food (Samhain, October 31).

The eight Sabbats commemorate an ancient and endless cycle of rebirth, cleansing, fertility, passion, growth, sacrifice, harvest, and death. Within that cycle can be seen yet another symbolic "yin/yang"—the light, or waxing year (Yule through Midsummer) and the dark, or waning year (Midsummer through Yule).

Celebrating these annual events gave our ancestors an opportunity to gather in community, to give thanks for surviving another winter, to bless the newborn calves in the fields and the wheat on the threshing floor, and to sing and dance the rhythm of their lives. Today, Wiccans gather in community to mark these days, to give thanks for all our blessings, and to reestablish our connection to the Earth and to all who have danced before us.

Most modern Witches celebrate the Sabbats on the exact dates, to align with the powerful symbolic and astrological energies inherent in each event. For others, juggling jobs and families means scheduling their festivities within a few days as a matter of convenience, but on the Sabbat taking a moment out of their lunch hour, or while the baby's napping, to connect to and honor Mother Earth. The word *Sabbat* means "to rest," and customarily these holidays are a time of observance rather than of magic-working. But this too can vary depending upon Tradition or personal preference, and many a powerful spell has been offered up to the starry heavens on a moonlit Midsummer's eve!

Along with the early agricultural and pastoral meanings of these holidays there is a circle of myth within the Wheel that follows the God and Goddess through all their days on the Earth. Because Wicca combines so many different Traditions and cultures, that myth has many tellings.

One version speaks of the Goddess giving birth to a son, the God, at Yule. Imbolc finds the Goddess resting and the God as a growing boy; at Ostara, the Goddess comes forth fully from her sleep, the God is strong and lusty, and the Earth is a splendor of green. At Beltane, the God has become a man, and he and the Goddess fall in love and unite. At Midsummer, the God's strength reaches its zenith, and the Goddess is ripe with a mother's power, as her belly swells with child. At Lughnasadh, the God begins to wane, even as the Goddess carries him, growing, within her; at Mabon, the Goddess reigns and the God prepares to die, a willing sacrifice for the Earth and his people. At Samhain, the God's death is celebrated, and the world awaits his rebirth of the Goddess, once more, at Yule.

This particular story raises more than a few eyebrows within conservative religions, and has been used as one of the ways to "illustrate" the evils of the Pagan path. Incest between deities? And not only that, it's *celebrated?* Remember, this is myth, a symbolic interpretation of the spiral of life, and like any good fairy tale or legend it is allegorical, not literal.

In other versions of the tale, it is the Goddess who is celebrated: born at Yule, she is an infant at Imbolc, a child at Ostara, a young maiden discovering love at Beltane, the full and bountiful mother by Midsummer, a maturing woman at Lughnasadh, in menopause at Mabon, and the wise crone at Samhain. The God can be seen in his dual aspects as the Oak King, who reigns in the waxing year, and the Holly King, who defeats his twin at Midsummer and holds the waning half. There is also the legend of Persephone, who goes into the Underworld in the fall at Mabon and returns to her mother, Demeter, in the spring at Ostara, thus dividing the year by

seasons of barrenness and fertility. And various other God and
Goddess myths celebrated in different Traditions explain the
changing seasons. More simply, the year can be divided by the
"Goddess time," which is the waxing year, and the "God time,"
which is the waning year.

There is no true "beginning" to the Wheel, and no end. It
continues to turn without cease, ever changing yet always the
same—at once mysterious, and blessedly familiar. By observing
the eight points of transition represented by the Sabbats, we are
pulled into the deeper mysteries of our planet and our people;
we become instinctual again, attuned to the world around us
and to our place in the circle. By ritualizing the life passages of
the Earth, and of the God and Goddess, we come to understand
our own: the cycles of our bodies, our relationships, our career
paths, our spiritual lives. We learn that change is empowering,
not fearsome; that for everything there is its opposite, and that
all will come round again, full circle, without fail.

## THE TURNING OF THE WHEEL

I invite you now to take a journey with me through a full turn
of the symbolic Wheel. Each of the Sabbats has a clear and distinct message, a tale to tell of the Earth, and of wonder; each
can be ritualized a hundred different ways. Here, I offer you a
spark of that wonder, a glance through a snow-frosted window,

a glint of August moonlight, a drop of May wine . . . a chance to feel whatever edge of wild is left in this world, and a few magical ways to claim it.

### Yule—December 20–23

We begin in the heart of the darkness. Winter is full upon the Earth; snow veils the landscape, thin trees are brittle with ice, and stars shatter the black mirror of the sky. The air is cold, metallic, sharp to breathe; scarves of woodsmoke drift in the sky over rooftops outlined with twinkling lights, and porch lamps gleam from early in the afternoon until long into the night.

It is the Winter Solstice, known also as Yule or Yuletide, the longest night of the year. In some Traditions, this night begins the new year; for all, this is the holy night of rebirth, when the Wheel begins to turn once more toward the light. In ancient times, people gathered on this night by a hearth, ablaze with fire, every windowsill and table dancing with candle flame— sympathetic magic to call the Sun back to the dark Earth, and welcome him.

Yule is a time of awakening, of welcoming the new and the possible, when the Sun is born again of the virgin Goddess. Evergreens, cut from the forest and brought into the home, are an ancient Celtic symbol that life continues, even in darkest winter; mistletoe is a Druid symbol of fertility, lovers, and the seed of the God. Holly and ivy invoke protection and good fortune; reindeer symbolize the Horned God; and the colors red, green, silver, and gold represent fire, earth, the Moon, and the Sun, respectively.

Customs for this Sabbat include burning a Yule log (an oak or birch log decorated with ribbons, greenery, and holly berries) to represent the fire of the returning Sun. Light the log using an unburned piece of the previous year's log; afterward, spread the ashes in your garden for fertility and save a small piece of the log for next year, keeping it in your home for good luck.

Burn bayberry candles for prosperity, or write wishes on bay leaves and throw them into the fire. Bake cookies or bread using cinnamon, a traditional spice representing the Sun. Make a wreath to symbolize the Wheel of the Year, and decorate it with pinecones to represent the God and fruit to represent the Goddess. Decorate a Yule tree with images to invoke the coming year's blessings, such as fruit and nuts for abundance, heart-shaped charms for love, feathers for inspiration, and coins for prosperity.

Write a list of all the things you wish to see "birthed" in the coming year, and tuck the list into a special box or container. (I use a beautiful little hand-carved wooden chest I found in an antique shop.) Leave the box undisturbed until next Yule, then open it and read your list. You'll be astonished to find that most, if not all, of your desires will have manifested! Just be careful what you wish for...

Stay up and watch the sunrise, and toast the returning Sun King with hot ginger-spiced cider.

Winter fights valiantly to hold the land. The crisp snows of January have turned to storms of sleet, and the Earth and the sky are gray, leaden, and heavy with the cold. But here and there, scattered like jewels in the sodden grass and the frozen garden, the first slender tips of daffodils start up toward the pale, growing Sun, and something in us stirs as well, as life pulses unseen beneath the still-slumbering ground.

This is Imbolc, known also as Imbolg, Candlemas, the Festival of Brighid (pronounced *Breed*), and the Feast of Lights. The word *Imbolc* means "in the belly," or in the womb of Mother Earth, as well as "in milk," which refers to ewes coming into milk for the first lambs of the season.

This Sabbat marks the return of spring, even as winter continues its reign. In ancient times, people honored the Goddess Brigid in her guise as the waiting bride of the youthful Sun God. A modern tradition at this Sabbat is "Groundhog's Day," based on an old British rhyme that says "If Candlemas Day be bright and clear, there'll be two winters in the year."

Imbolc is a time of cleansing and purification, for discarding outworn things of the passing year in preparation for the warm spring days ahead and to make room in our lives for the Earth's new bounty. Rites of initiation and consecration of altars and ritual tools are often conducted at this Sabbat.

Candle wreaths or wheels are traditional, as the Sun is seen as a candle flame at Imbolc, compared to the balefire of his power at Midsummer. Grain dollies are representative of the Goddess Bride, and wishing wells and still, deep pools are the domain of the Goddess this day. Lavender, white, silver, and red are traditional colors; amethyst and quartz crystals are symbolic as well.

The customs of Imbolc include ritual "spring cleaning" of the house, to banish the last vestiges of winter and hasten the growing days. Use lavender and rosemary in a pot of boiling water to wash floors and walls, vinegar and mugwort for windows and mirrors. Burn sage to cleanse the psychic energies, and replace old protection and prosperity charms.

Cleanse your body with a ritual bath scented with lavender, and as you soak, meditate to clear your mind and heart of any thoughts or emotions that no longer serve you. Make hand-dipped candles, write Goddess-inspired poetry, paint, make a collage, or do any other hands-on craft to symbolize the germination of life and ideas. Wish upon a coin or a crystal, then throw it into a still body of deep water and ask the water spirits to bless and guard your desires until they manifest.

Just before sunset, turn off all the lights in the house. With a single white candle burning to represent Brighid, knock three times on the front door and invite the Goddess to enter, asking that she bestow health, success, abundance, and love upon everyone in the house. Then slowly begin turning on the lights, moving room to room, until every light in the house is on.

Milk-white clouds pillow in an agate sky. Buds swell tightly against slender branches, and soft, mousy catkins beg to be patted by children on their way to school. Fresh rain breaks over the greening Earth, scattering the petals of cherry blossoms like confetti at a birthday party, and there's a brave new slant to the sunlight coming through the kitchen window at daybreak.

This is the Spring Equinox, known also as Ostara, or Eostar. It's the time of balance, when light and dark are equal and the Earth swells with new life. In ancient times, people celebrated the arrival of spring, and the Goddess Eostar, or Eostre, whose symbols were the egg and the hare, both representations of the Great Mother.

Ostara is a festival of fertility and resurrection, the union of sun and soil, a time of planting, mothering, and tending to young children and animals. At the Spring Equinox, the God and the Goddess are now equals, and they dance together across the Earth. Wherever they step, flowers appear and bloom beneath their feet, and sorrow turns to delight as the world is reborn.

Traditional symbols of this Sabbat are eggs, lambs, chicks, and rabbits—all symbolic of the Goddess in her "mother" aspect. Eggs are considered a symbol of the universe itself, with the shell representing earth; the membrane, air; the yolk, fire; and the white, water. An ancient Ostara custom was to dye eggs red, the color of life-force and regeneration. Other traditional colors of this Sabbat are silver and penny-candy pastels.

Celebrate Ostara with fresh spring flowers, bouquets of freesia, daffodils, lilac, and tulips, and herbs such as clover, lemongrass, and mint.

Make "oracle eggs." Draw magical symbols on hard-boiled eggs with paraffin or white crayon. These can include astrological signs, runes, and dream symbology. Have an egg hunt; drop the eggs into pots of dye, and divine your future by the symbols that appear.

Water your houseplants with rainwater that has been steeped overnight in the light of a full Moon. Play favorite childhood games. Blow bubbles, play hopscotch and jacks, and jump rope using affirmations as rhyme. Bless the seeds for your garden, and envision health, happiness, and prosperity growing for you in the warmth of the Sun.

## Beltane—May 1

Sunlight dapples the forest floor. A copper fox appears through the gloaming, then vanishes again with one sweet, sharp bark, an invitation to follow him into the fanciful weave of light and shadow. There is a wildness in the air, a spice that belongs to more than lilacs or the sweet woodruff blooming beneath the trees. Ferns glisten with morning dew, and somewhere, lovers conspire to meet at sundown, to bless the fields of summer with their passion.

It is Beltane, known also as Bealtaine, May Day, and Walpurgisnacht, which means "Night of the Witches." It is the festival of passion, one of the two greatest Sabbats in the Pagan year, second only to Samhain, which lies directly opposite it on the Wheel.

In ancient times, Beltane (named for Bel, the Celtic God of Light) was traditionally begun on the eve of April 30, when great bonfires were lit using bundles of nine different woods sacred to the Druids. These fires had healing properties; herds of cattle were driven between them and people would jump through the flames to ensure purity and protection.

Beltane is perhaps best known as a celebration of sexuality and fertility. Starhawk, author of *Spiral Dance,* describes this Sabbat as a night when "sweet desire weds wild delight." All-night trysts in the forests between young lovers, called "greenwood marriages," were common magical practice on Beltane of old, and children conceived of these arrangements were known as "merry-begets," and were considered children of the gods. The Maypole is an ancient symbol of the Great Rite, the sexual union of the God and the Goddess, celebrated by lovers everywhere on May eve.

Other symbols of this Sabbat include May baskets, flowered chaplets worn in ritual, and bowls of May wine—white wine, strawberry liqueur, fresh strawberries, and sprigs of woodruff harvested at dawn.

Celebrate this Sabbat with bright, fresh colors, especially red and white, considered traditional for the ribbons of the Maypole. A tall, straight, branchless tree or a flagpole, as many rib-

bons as there are dancers, bells at your wrists and heels, and
merry music weave the May!

Wake before the sunrise and wash your face with dew, ensur-
ing beauty throughout the year. Hang baskets of flowers, fruits,
and baked goods from trees for your own enjoyment and con-
sumption throughout the day as well as for the wildlife.

Create a Beltane "bower," an isolated hideaway for the celebrations of love. A tent or pavilion outdoors, or any room of
the house, will do—decorate it with candles, music, pillows,
incense, flowers, ribbons, and any other sensual accoutrements.

Build your own Beltane fire of nine different woods, then
leap over it to purify and cleanse yourself of unwanted things.
Or, if space does not permit a bonfire, create a smaller blaze and
write what you wish to eliminate on colorful ribbons of paper,
then burn them to ash in the flames.

## Midsummer—June 20–23

Nights are warm, and stars shimmer in the sky like a blacktop
road in the noonday sun. Roses spill over garden gates, heavy
with bees and perfume; field and forest are lush and teeming
with life. Faerie-folk gather in the woodland glades, and frolic
beside moss-banked streams; the fires of summer burn green
and gold, and everywhere there is high magic afoot!

It is Midsummer's Eve, known also as Litha and the Summer
Solstice, the longest day of the year. This is the Sun God at his
mightiest, the height of his reign, and also the very moment

when he begins his decline, as the days give way in the coming months to darkness. In ancient times, people celebrated the power of the Sun and his love for the Goddess, now pregnant with his child. The Earth's bounty spills over in every garden patch and shimmering field; Midsummer is a festival of growth and glory—even as the God begins to wane, his light will be transformed within the womb of the Earth as the fruits and grains of the coming harvest.

Midsummer is also when the realm of faerie is most astir. Faerie magic is powerful, mischievous, and, at times, unpredictable, so take care when working spells this night! At this Sabbat, fire is the key element, and symbols include solar wheels (an equilateral cross within a circle), the dark, curving feathers of a rooster's tail, and jars full of honey, the gold of the Sun.

The colors of Midsummer are greens and gold, and fire colors such as crimson, orange, yellow, and bronze. Handfastings, or Pagan marriage ceremonies, are commonly held at Midsummer, and spells of transformation and purpose are often performed. Other customs include lighting a ritual bonfire, sprinkling it with magical herbs, and dancing round the flames, asking for the blessings of health and prosperity.

Harvest your magical herbs on Midsummer morning, using a special ritual knife just for this purpose, and hang them to dry for use in spellwork in the coming months. Catch a jar of fireflies, whose green glow represents faerie fire deep in the heart of the forest. Make wishes upon the tiny creatures, and just before dawn, release them to carry on their natural business and to carry your wishes to the Goddess.

Put out gifts of food and libation for the faeries. Fresh milk or cream, butter, wine, cakes, and honey are all much desired sustenance in the realm of Faerie. Gifts of coins, ribbon, or colorful stones are also fancied. Leave your offerings in the garden, near a stream or pond, or beneath the bracken fern at the edge of the woods.

Decorate a wooden wheel with crimson and yellow paint, gold ribbons, and bright sun-colored flowers. Roll it down a slope at sunset, or, if conditions permit, set the wheel ablaze and send it downhill into a pond or lake to hail the glory of the Sun King and the beginning of the waning year.

## Lughnasadh—August 1

The summer air is hot and still, the afternoon hazy; crickets call relentlessly from among the brown grasses, and ears of corn are the same heavy, burnished gold as the late-day sun. Hawks circle in the blue-white sky overhead, and seedpods ripen where flowers bloomed just a month before. But shadows begin to lengthen along the garden wall, and the nights come, just a bit cooler, perhaps; a settling begins in the Earth, a gathering, a slow, quiet turning toward the coming darkness.

It is Lughnasadh (pronounced *loo-na-sa*), known also as Lammas, or Lammastide, the first of the three harvest festivals on the Wheel of the Year. Named for Lugh the Long Handed, a

Celtic God of light and fire, this Sabbat marks the ending of summer and the first harvest of the grain. In ancient times the God of Grain, or John Barleycorn as legend knows him, sacrificed himself so that the people would have plenty of food for the coming winter. In some Traditions, the Goddess becomes the Reaper, and presides over the passing of the God, who willingly gives his life to bless the harvest.

Lughnasadh is a time of giving thanks for summer's bounty, and of completion, and of finishing projects begun in the spring. It is also a time of ritual housecleaning in preparation for the nesting energies of fall and winter. Symbols of this Sabbat include sheaves of grain, garlic braids, sunflowers, and corn. The colors of Lughnasadh are the golds and dusky hues of the turning Earth.

Celebrate this time by feasting on fresh corn, vegetables, and berries, thanking the God for his transformation into the soul of the harvest. Ritually "sacrifice" negative thoughts, emotions, or behaviors. Make garlic or onion braids, and hang them in the kitchen to ward off disease.

Go to a farmers' market or medieval fair and enjoy the "first fruits" of the local artists and growers. Lammastide was the traditional season for craft festivals in medieval times, when merchants would decorate their market stands with bright squares of silk and lengths of colored ribbon, and hold contests of arms and ceremonial dances. Contact your local Society for Creative Anachronism to find out what fun might be afoot in your area!

Harvest herbs from the garden, and make flavored oils and vinegars to keep a taste of summer in your pantry all winter long. Ritually bake and bless a special loaf of bread, using grains native to your home, and share the bounty of the first harvest with family and loved ones.

### Mabon—September 20–23

Mist blankets the morning garden and the empty fields; a last rose blooms slowly over the arbor by the backyard gate. Paintbox leaves fall to the ground under galoshes and the wheels of slicker-yellow school buses. Sweaters come out of cedar chests, soup pots simmer, and wild geese make their mercurial journey southward across the pale autumn sky.

It is the Autumn Equinox, known also as Mabon and Harvest Home. This is the second harvest festival, a time of rejoicing and thanksgiving, a time on the Earth when, again, night and day are in equal balance. In ancient times, people took a respite from their labors in the orchards and fields at this Sabbat, giving thanks for the Earth's bounty with feasts and offerings of wine and apples.

At Mabon, the Wheel turns toward endings, and the light wanes more noticeably each day. Larders are stocked, blankets are aired and mended, and the last of summer's riches are canned, preserved, and stored against winter's chill. Now is a time for rest, reflection, and for completing anything left undone in the warm season's wake. Symbols of Mabon include grapevines, gourds, cornucopias, and the bright scattered leaves of autumn trees.

Celebrate this Sabbat with the reds, golds, rusts, and browns of the Earth, and thin yellow candles to ward off the coming dark. Break out the good china, the finest silver, and the creamiest linens, and prepare a hearty feast for friends and loved ones, made with the freshest offerings from autumn's table.

Host or attend a wine-tasting party in honor of Dionysus, Roman God of Wine, who is traditionally celebrated at the Autumn Equinox. Harvest the last of the vegetables and herbs from your garden, and gather and bless the seeds for next spring. Make apple butter, berry jams, and fresh-pressed cider; have a hayride or host a barn dance to bid the summer farewell.

Harvest gourds and dry them to make ritual rattles. Paint them with magical symbols, then fill them with sand, pebbles, or dried corn and decorate the ends with strips of leather or suede strung with feathers, shells, and colorful beads.

Spend some time meditating on all you have accomplished in the past months, and write out a list of all you have to be thankful for. Gratitude is powerful medicine—keep the list where you can refer to it, if ever you begin to feel a bit "grinchy" during the coming winter.

## Samhain—October 31

A white lace of frost webs the sidewalk kaleidoscope of leaves. Hillsides are ablaze with flame-colored trees, fields lie fallow and dark, and cornstalks dry to the color of bone in the low golden sun. The sky promises rain tonight and winds rise to torture the clouds. Fog swirls down the darkened street, shrouding the candlelit grin of a glowing jack-o'-lantern, and the veil between the land of the living and the land of the dead grows as thin and insubstantial as the mist.

It is Samhain (pronounced *sow-en*), known also as All Hallow's Eve or Halloween. This is the third harvest festival of the year, a time to honor our departed loved ones and the night when, in legend, the spirits of the dead return to commune with the living. The God has died, returning to the Underworld to await his rebirth at Yule; the Goddess is the Crone, mourning her lost love, leaving the world for a time in darkness.

In ancient times, people slaughtered cattle at Samhain, leaving the breeding stock alive for the following spring, each year wondering if there would be food enough to survive the coming winter. They celebrated despite the fear—balefires burned on every hillside, great feasts were held, and places were set at the table for the spirits who walked the Earth. For the Celts, this was New Year's Eve; in some traditions, Samhain marked a "time out of time," the ending of the old year, the new year not beginning until the Sun's rebirth at Yule.

Samhain is considered the oldest and most sacred of the Sabbats; opposite Beltane on the Wheel of the Year, these two high holy days honor death and life in their unending spiral. Symbols of this Sabbat include the cauldron, which represents the womb of the Goddess, brooms, masks, skeletons, pomegranates, and, of course, jack-o'-lanterns. The colors of Samhain are late autumn rusts, scarlets, browns, and golds, as well as black for protection and orange for the power of fire.

Customs of this Sabbat are ancient and include the "Dumb Supper," setting a place for the silent souls of departed loved ones at your table and lighting their way to your hearth with carved pumpkins and candlelight.

Make masks to wear and to decorate your doorway. Masks were used to confuse or frighten away unwanted spirits in times past; today, make them gaudy and glittery, using fabric, feathers, beads, and trinkets to honor the many faces of the Goddess and the God.

Carve a grinning jack-o'-lantern and place it on the front porch or walkway to welcome friendly souls and protect your home from mischievous ones, as our ancestors did long ago.

All forms of divination are paramount on Samhain Eve. Dark mirrors for scrying ("seeing" psychically or mentally), Tarot cards, runes, or pendulums are all perfect tools for utilizing the heightened spiritual energies at this Sabbat. More playful means of divining are derived from Victorian Samhain celebrations. For example, to discover the identity of your true love, peel an apple in one long strip, let it fall to the ground, and read the initials in the bends and curves; or put acorns in front of the fire, name each, and wait to see which one pops first.

Leave your favorite candy out for all the visiting "spirits," as people left food and wine on the stoop for the faerie folk and the wandering souls on Samhain of old.

Contemplate the coming winter, and use this time out of time to let die old ways of thinking, outworn beliefs, and negative patterns. Meditate, rest, and incorporate relaxation techniques over the next weeks to deepen your psychic awareness and to restore your soul. And await your own rebirth at Yule, as the Wheel comes round full circle once again.

In a Witch's year, holidays are rhythmic, magical, sublime. They make sense, and the spirit finds *you*. Winter seems far less daunting when you celebrate the return of light in the heart of the darkness. And the dog days of summer seem tamer when you realize that the Sun's mighty force wanes a little more with the passing of each day. On the Wheel of the Year, every Earth change is a celebration, and every celebration is an opportunity to strengthen your connection to yourself, your people, your planet, and your God.

# five

# THE WITCH'S MOON:
# LUNAR CELEBRATIONS

*Mother of this unfathomable world...*
*I have watched thy shadow*
*and the darkness of thy steps*
*And my heart ever gazed on*
*the depth of thy deep mysteries.*

—Percy Bysshe Shelley

Of all that is mysterious, and wondrous, and magical about Wicca, the most powerful of all is the Moon. Since ancient times, people have looked to the Moon to define the order of their days. The Sun's cycle could only dictate the passing of the seasons; people needed a way to mark time in smaller increments. The first calendars, therefore, were lunar, the division of weeks and months decided by the Moon's waxing and waning phases. The Chinese philosophy of yin and yang is based on these same principles, and both Muslim and Jewish cultures still divide their years by the Moon's cycle.

The tangible nature of the Moon's energy is indisputable. Ocean tides, spawning fish, earthquakes, and catastrophic weather phenomena have all been studied in direct correlation to the Moon's cyclical temper. Since emotions correspond to the element of water, just as the tides are braced and buffeted by the Moon's influence so too is the human psyche. Research done by psychiatrists, police investigators, and hospitals show dramatic fluctuations in criminal and psychotic behaviors during both the Full and New Moon phases. But the effects are not purely negative; heightened psychic and intuitive awareness, precognitive dreams, and enhanced healing and manifestation ability are all gifts of the Moon's watery spirit.

Women have always been the most aware of, and thus most profoundly connected to, the Moon's unique energies, as the path of the Moon is a celestial illustration of the menstrual cycle. Because of this instinctual connection, women were the healers and the sages in the clans of our ancestors as well as the keepers of the calendar, charting the most auspicious times for planting, harvesting, gatherings, and ritual. For this same connection, the Moon is seen as the Goddess, changing in her monthly circle as do women's bodies; the cycle of increased hormone production, ovulation, and menses in women corresponding exactly to the Maiden (New), Mother (Full), and Crone (Dark) phases of the Moon.

So. What does all of this mean to a Witch? In a word, *magic*. The Craft, with its reverence for the feminine, has always been irrevocably linked to the mystical influence of the Moon. Alongside the eight Sabbats on the Wheel of the Year, Witches also celebrate Esbats, or lunar holidays, each month when the Moon is full. Esbats are the "working" holidays of the Craft. Each Moon phase has a distinct energy that can be tapped for specific magical purposes; many Witches observe both New and Full Moon Esbats, and work magic in between as well, according to need. The word *Esbat* literally means "to frolic," and there is merriment aplenty whenever Witches gather to celebrate in the glow of the Goddess.

## THE THREE FACES OF THE MOON

As with all forms of energy, the effect created through magic is based entirely upon the intent with which the energy is used. Magic is the conscious and focused use of natural forces; the phases of the Moon offer powerful opportunities to create positive energetic outcomes.

**New Moon:** During this period, the Moon comes out from her hiding place as the Dark Crone, and begins to show herself as the Maiden, a thin slip of light in the eastern sky. Some Witches call this phase "Diana's Bow," referring to the Goddess Diana, Mistress of the Hunt, and her celestial longbow. Now is the time to bless and begin new projects, anything that requires energy to grow, such as gardens, business ventures, new homes, or educational pursuits. Personal growth and healing are accented, as is "attraction magic"—drawing something to you, such as love, abundance, health, or success—and if done well, you can expect to see results by the next Full Moon. The New Moon is also a time for divination of all kinds, spells of spiritual intention, and for any creative project you wish to see birthed, with magical results.

The phase between the New and the Full Moon is called the Waxing Moon, and anything involving growth and positive change is highlighted now.

**Full Moon:** Here is the Mother in all her glory, sailing high in the heavens, trailing silvery skirts across the bright Earth. Magic that calls forth personal power, abundance, protection, fertility, and psychic awareness is the most fruitful during this time. Cleansing of ritual tools, crystals, Tarot decks, and the like can also be done now. The power of this phase can be accessed for a period of seven days—three days prior to, the night of, and three days after the Full Moon. Magic worked during the Full Moon often takes one complete Moon cycle to come to fruition.

The Full Moon is also the time to honor the Goddess. We do this in the Craft by "Drawing Down the Moon," a ritual that brings the Moon's power directly into the physical body. Done well, a Drawing fills you with the most extraordinary energy— tingling, electrified, alive, your senses heightened, the air fairly

crackling around you. And any ritual magic worked after
embodying the Goddess in this way is practically guaranteed to
catch the universe's attention.

The phase between the Full and the New Moon is called the
Waning Moon. Here, banishings are performed; anything you
wish to release or reject can be successfully dealt with during
this period. Negative emotion, illness, habits, or addiction can
be given the magical "boot" as the Moon thins and grows hun-
gry, becoming once again the Dark Crone.

**Dark Moon:** The three days before the New Moon, the Goddess goes into hiding, not showing herself at all in the heavens,
leaving the Earth in darkness. This is a period of rest, meditation, vision questing, and respite from magical workings. However, in the event of a necessary banishing or ending, the
Goddess Hecate is most present at this time to assist.

## MOON MAGIC

There are thirteen Full Moons in a calendar year, due to the
rotation of the Earth, and each has a number of ancient names
and magical meanings. Here are just a few of those correspondences:

**January:** Known as the Wolf Moon, Chaste Moon, or Cold
Moon, this is a time for beginnings, conception, protection

spells, and working on goals and issues that are personal in nature.

**February:** Ice Moon, Storm Moon, or Wild Moon. This is a time for growth and future plans, purification, cleansing, healing, self-love, and acceptance.

**March:** Seed Moon, Plow Moon, or Crow Moon. This is a time for balance, growth, exploration, cultivation, and prosperity.

**April:** Hare Moon, Pink Moon, or Planting Moon. This is a time for creativity, manifestation, self-confidence, acting on opportunity, and love magic.

**May:** Merry Moon, Flower Moon, or Dyad Moon. This is a time for intuition, faerie lore, "green" magic, and connecting with nature spirits.

**June:** Mead Moon, Honey Moon, or Lovers' Moon. This is a time for protection, making decisions, personal strength, and fertility.

**July:** Hay Moon, Thunder Moon, or Blessing Moon. This is a time for divination, dreams, focusing on goals, and expanding spiritual consciousness.

**August:** Corn Moon, Barley Moon, or Wyrt (green plant) Moon. This is a time for health and vitality, family, friends, and gathering.

**September:** Harvest Moon, Wine Moon, or Singing Moon. This is a time for completion, organization, balance, and letting go of worn-out things, ideas, or emotions.

**October:** Blood Moon, Falling Leaf Moon, or Moon of the Changing Seasons. This is a time for transition, release, inner peace, past lives, and karmic completion.

**November:** Snow Moon, Mourning Moon, or Moon of Storms. This is a time for going inward, rest and preparation, transformation, and spiritual communion.

**December:** Oak Moon, Long Night's Moon, or Winter Moon. This is a time for acknowledging death and rebirth, darkness, your spiritual journey, and all those in need on planet Earth.

The thirteenth Full Moon of the year is called the Blue Moon, and occurs as the second of two Full Moons in a given calendar month. The Blue Moon is a powerful time for setting long-term goals, acknowledging accomplishments, prophesizing, divination, and past-life regression.

There are also specific ways to work with the astrological aspects of the Moon's phases, such as the Moon in Aries being a good time to plant magical herbs or cultivate talents and abilities, and the Moon in Virgo being the ideal energy for discipline, healing, and the intuitive arts. Check sources such as *Llewellyn's Magical Almanac* and *The Witches' Almanac* for more detail on the Moon in each sign.

# six

# CASTING THE CIRCLE: SACRED SPACE AND MAGICAL TOOLS

*Wisdom begins with wonder.*

—Socrates

There is a place where magic exists, always. A place where time seems to stand still, where the mundane and the worldly are automatically checked at the door, where the very air around you is inherently sacred. A place where, no matter what may be happening in your world—no matter the traffic, or the dust on the coffee table, or the kids, or the dog, or the leaky pipe under the laundry room sink—you can shed the cares of the human experience for a time, and be utterly transformed by Spirit.

Where is this place, you ask? A Buddhist monastery on an isolated peak in the Himalayas? Some imaginary island in the middle of a dreamer's sea? In the Craft, this place can be found in any living room or backyard, or in any corner of anyone's bedroom. This place is the magic circle and, for a Witch, it is truly sacred space.

Created by "casting," or drawing in the air with focused energy, the circle is a portable temple, the place where ritual is presented, spells are worked, magical energy is raised, and where a Witch becomes one with his or her chosen deities. Done well, it is a full-blown sensory experience, a visible, tangible, living sphere of physical power.

A circle can be cast literally anywhere. Inside, or out; in a room designated only for ritual space, or in the kitchen, round the dining table, with the chairs pulled back or stacked in the hall. Some Traditions insist that the circle be exactly nine feet in diameter (nine being the number of the Goddess) and cast with very specific layers of element and word. I have cast circles just big enough to encompass my physical body and personal altar space, and I have participated at coven celebrations where the circle fit some fifty pagan revelers, with room left over to dance! Some Witches cast circles only for working spells; others include their Sabbat celebrations within the magical boundary. I have cast circles for everything, even for a period of time turning my bed at night into sacred space to help combat a sleeping problem I was experiencing.

In a moment, I'll show you how to conjure such a space. But before the circle come the tools that help create the magic, and in the heart of the circle, the Witch's altar—the place where magic begins.

The altar is a physical point of ritual focus, containing items sacred and essential to a Witch's magic and faith. The altar can be anything from a beautiful antique side table to a simple board set across two TV trays. It can be permanent or portable. Most Witches have more than one altar in their homes—one or two fixed shrines to honor Spirit or their chosen deities, and then the working altar for ritual and magical purposes.

Shrines can be any size, as small as a windowsill, a shelf, or the corner of a dresser if that is all the space available or required. The working altar, set up in the center of the circle for ritual, should be large enough to accommodate whatever spell or celebration is at hand, much like needing ample kitchen counter space when you're conjuring a holiday feast.

The altar is traditionally laid out with the Goddess, or the feminine, on the left side, and the God, or the masculine, on the right. This relates to the placement of the Witch's magical tools, ceremonial objects that help direct the energy used in spells and ritual.

## MAGICAL TOOLS

Following is a list of the most common magical tools used in the Craft. Wicca can certainly be practiced without these objects, for they contain no power other than that which we give them. But like anything symbolic or sacred in nature, a

Witch's tools serve to enhance our ritual abilities, strengthen our connection to our religion, and become a precious part of us through touch, intent, and time.

**The Athame:** Sometimes called the magic knife, ritual dagger, or sword, the athame is used to direct and manipulate the energy raised in ritual and spellwork. Most often the athame's blade is dull, as it is not used for cutting, and double-edged; many Traditions stipulate that the handle be black or dark in color, as black absorbs power. The athame represents the God and the element of fire, and so is traditionally placed on the right side of the altar.

**The Bolline:** A knife used for cutting things in ritual such as wands, herbs, or cords, and for inscribing symbols in candles or other ritual tools. Traditionally, the bolline's blade is curved and the handle white to distinguish it from the athame, and it too represents the God, or the male energy.

**Book of Shadows:** The Book of Shadows is a Witch's record of all things magical in his or her life and practice. Researched information; facts about crystals, herbs, astrology, etc.; the phases of the Moon; poetry and magical quotes; wisdom gleaned from other books and other Witches; and, of course, spells and rituals. Keeping a record of how a ritual was performed and the outcome of magical workings helps you refine and expand on your abilities.

Anything and everything related to your Craft experience is material for your Book of Shadows. Your book can be as simple or as elaborate as you wish. There are beautiful art-quality blank books or journals available on the market, but a good old-fashioned three-ring binder will do very nicely.

**The Broom:** Perhaps the most symbolic of a Witch's tools, at least in the public eye, the broom is used for both spellworking and ritual, for "sweeping" the ritual area clean of negative energy, for laying on the ground as a physical doorway to the circle, and for jumping over in Beltane or Pagan marriage ceremonies.

Handmade brooms, preferably round as opposed to flat, can be found at craft fairs, farmers' markets, and harvest festivals. Some Witches collect brooms, and most name them, as the broom is a symbol of the female Witch and has a definite quality of an inanimate "familiar," or kindred spirit.

**Candles:** Candles are one of the simplest yet most powerful of magical tools. They contain all four of the elements—earth (solid wax), air (oxygen to feed the flame), water (melted wax), and fire. Candlelight transforms a room with mystical ambience, and a candle that has been charged, or instilled with magical intent, carries that intent to the heavens on its dancing flame.

Magical candles are chosen for color property, and "dressed"—anointed with an appropriate oil (such as cinnamon for prosperity, or rose for love) and carved with runes, symbols, or words that claim the spell's purpose—before use. A magical candle should be allowed to burn down completely. If the flame must be put out, snuff it—never blow it out, as this can "blow away" the intention of the spell!

**The Cauldron:** The cauldron, another image linked inexorably with Witchcraft, is the ultimate symbol of the Goddess, literally the womb of life, the tomb of death, and the legendary rebirth of the phoenix from the ashes. Cauldrons are traditionally made of cast iron, with three legs, and come in many sizes. Placed on the altar, if space permits, or on the floor to the left, they are used ritually to hold earth or water in spring rites, or fire in the winter to represent the returning Sun, held in the belly of the Goddess. The cauldron can also be used for mixing oils and potions, divination by scrying with still water, and for burning parchment scrolls and written spells, sending your wishes to the Goddess on the flames.

Cauldrons can be a bit hard to come by, but well worth the search, as they tend to show up quite magically. You can find them through certain mail-order sources, but those are usually brand new, and there's something to be said about the energy of history that tends to collect in certain symbolic objects.

**The Censor:** Also known as a thurible, or incense burner, the censor represents the elements of fire and air, and is often placed near the center of the altar. This is a tool used to purify the ritual area, and to help achieve full sensory connection to the magic being performed. There are many different styles of burners available, and hundreds of varieties of incense. Different fragrances of incense have different meanings, and are used accordingly for the type of ritual or spell being conducted, such as spicy scents for prosperity, flower scents for love, and herbal varieties for healing (see Scott Cunningham's *The Complete Book of Incense, Oils and Brews* for a comprehensive list).

**The Chalice:** The chalice is symbolic of the Goddess, fertility, and the waters of emotion. In legend, it harkens back to the Holy Grail that restored Camelot and brought forth the rebirth of England. In ritual, the chalice is used to hold Holy Water for blessing and consecrating; for the drinking of wine, cider, or ale at the end of a ceremony; and for enacting the Great Rite, the lowering of the athame into the chalice, representing the union of the God and Goddess. The chalice is traditionally long stemmed, of any food-safe material you desire, and is placed on the left side of the altar, for the feminine.

**The Pentacle:** Another symbol of Witchcraft that is steeped in ancient ceremony, the pentacle is a flat disk inscribed with a pentagram, the five-pointed star within a circle that has been used magically as protection and invocation for centuries. Traditionally placed in the center of the altar, with the star in the upright position, the pentacle represents the element of earth, with the five points of the star representing fire, water, earth, air, and spirit, respectively. Commonly made of wood, metal, wax, or clay, the pentacle is used for consecrating and empowering tools, amulets, crystals, jewelry, and other objects by placing them in the center of the star during ritual.

**Symbols of Deity:** Candles are customary to represent the deities—green or silver for the Goddess and red or gold for the God, placed at the head of the altar. Statues, symbols of the Moon and Sun, and other token objects, such as seashells or feathers for the Goddess and stones or a deer antler for the God, can also be used.

**Symbols of the Elements:** The four directions are also represented on the working altar with their corresponding elements, to align with the powers of nature during ritual. For north, the direction of earth, salt, crystals, a bowl of soil, figures of a bear, wolf, or stag, or a small potted plant are all symbolic. South, which is fire, can be a candle, oil lamp, cactus, or the figure of a dragon, snake, or lion. For east, which is air, use a feather, incense, bell, or figures of birds or butterflies. West, which is water, can be a cup or bowl of water, seashells, or symbols of fish, dolphins, whales, or swans.

**The Wand:** Ah, yes. The infamous magic wand, with which Disney Witches zap people into toads and Disney fairy godmothers turn pumpkins into limo rides to meet Prince Charming. In the Craft, the wand is one of the primary projectors of energy, an instrument of invocation and healing used for casting and opening the circle. It is one of the most magically manifesting tools in the Witch's goody bag. There are countless stories of Witches searching high and low for the perfect branch to make the perfect wand, only to have one show up in the parking lot of the local mini-mart after a storm, or in the mouth of their neighbor's dog.

There are many schools of traditional thought regarding the procuring of a Witch's wand. Making one versus buying one. Harvesting a live branch versus finding one on the ground. Willow versus oak, versus cherry, etc. Beautiful wands can be found in metaphysical shops, some made of various sacred woods, others of copper or silver with crystal tips and elaborate ornamentation. As with all things in the Craft, use your instincts and your imagination. The wand is to be an extension of your own physical and energetic bodies; find one that *feels* right; better yet, let it find you.

Collecting your ritual tools is one of the most delightful sidelines of the Craft. Antique stores, gift boutiques, flea markets, garage sales, craft festivals, and junk shops are all fair territory on the quest, as are metaphysical shops, mail-order sources, and your own creative hands. Let the Goddess guide you, and prepare for magical happenings! Have a safe place in which to store your treasures once home—a trunk, dresser drawer, or a special cupboard are all good places to keep your tools when they are not accompanying you inside the sacred circle.

Once you have procured your tools, they should be cleansed to banish any negative energy they may have accumulated and consecrated (blessed and instilled with magical intent) *before you use them,* even if they are new. Ritual tools are conductors of energy; they absorb and vibrate with the essence of whomever or whatever has spent a significant time with them, and it is important to make them yours, magically and energetically, through and through. A ritual for cleansing and consecrating your ceremonial tools and objects can be found in chapter 10.

## CASTING THE CIRCLE

The circle is the prerequisite for all things magical. The rituals and spells outlined in the coming chapters will all be performed inside this sacred space. Your ritual tools will be cleansed and consecrated there, so until that is done, this exercise is just to get a feel for the enchantment that awaits you. Please remember that there are many different ways to do all the things we do in Witchcraft. The beauty of this religion is that there is no "one right way" to practice, worship, or believe. My way is just that—mine. I'm sharing it here for you to take what you like, in hopes that you will use it as a springboard to find other, better ways, or to create your own.

Stand facing North, at the outer edge of your ritual space. Take a deep, slow breath and close your eyes. Feel your feet, firmly on the ground. Raise your arms out to the side, and tilt your head back as if looking at the sky, as if you could take off from the ground and fly at any moment.

Imagine a pure white light streaming down from the heavens, from the God and Goddess themselves. It is tingly, effervescent, warm as blood. See it in your mind's eye, feel it against your face; let it flow down through the top of your head and fill your body. It ignites you, quickens you, makes your heart beat just a little bit faster.

Now, open your eyes, and using your right hand (the right hand is for projecting; the left for receiving), send the energy whirling about inside of you out through either your palm or your pointed index finger and into the air before you. See it, blue-white and electric, shooting from your hand. It leaves a mist, a shimmering frost of light, like a child's Fourth of July sparkler waved in the darkness. (Don't worry if at first you don't actually "see" the energy; *believe,* and the more you practice casting, the more your imagination will train your physical eyes to perceive.) It is with this laser of universal energy that you will draw the boundary of your magic circle.

Begin walking slowly to the right, or *deosil* (clockwise), sending the energy in a continuous stream before you, tracing a complete circle around the outside edge of your ritual area. Speak these words, or others of your own to the same effect, aloud:

> *I cast this circle once around*
> *All within by magic bound.*
> *A sacred space, a healing place,*
> *Safe from harm by Spirit's grace.*

When you have come round again to your starting point in the North, stand and raise your arms above you in a "V"; visualize the energy continuing to flow down from the heavens, into you, through you, and across the ritual space, creating a domed ceiling of light and pure protection. Extend the circle down through the floor, into the Earth, and fill it in beneath you so that your circle is now a perfect sphere of energy.

When the circle feels complete, stop and let the energy dissipate within you. Feel your body grow calm. Breathe. Sit down, or walk about inside the sanctuary you have made. The air shimmers. The boundary of the circle hums; put your hand to it, gently, and feel the life force beneath your fingers. Time lies suspended here, peaceful at your feet, and the God and Goddess are *alive*. You are between the worlds, held in sacred space, and only grace can come of it.

This is the time, in a formal ritual or spell, when you would invoke the deities, call the directions, and work your magic. For now, simply experience this place. Pray, or meditate, or just be. When you are ready, it is time to open the circle.

Stand in the North, as you did in the beginning, eyes closed, arms outstretched, face to heaven. This time, the energy you project should be like a sword—sharp and clean, piercing the veil, opening the circle once again to the human realm of physical time and space. Visualize the wall of energy separating, dissolving, whirling away like a mist from your outstretched hand; walk the boundary to the left, or *widdershins* (counterclockwise), and speak these words, or your own, aloud:

> *I part this circle, all is done,*
> *Magic forged by Moon and Sun.*
> *All who came here, thanks to thee*
> *To go in peace, and Blessed Be!*

Complete the circle, feeling the air become cool, seeing the light dissipate in a shower of sparks, like sulfur into dark water. Let the energy drain from you, gently, into Mother Earth; see it healing her, making her whole. Ground yourself, being aware of your breath, your heartbeat, your feet against the floor. It is finished. The circle is open, but never broken; there will always be a fine, glittering film of magic left behind when any Witch is done with sacred space.

A cast circle should stand undisturbed for the length of your rite or magical working. For this reason, it is good to plan your activities for a time when you know you won't be interrupted and in a place where your roommate or mother-in-law isn't likely to step across the threshold unaware. If the circle is accidentally broken, simply recast. But magic is best worked when the rhythm and the energy can be raised and explored without interference.

A cast circle should not, however, be a prison cell. If for some reason it is imperative you leave the ritual space, or someone needs to enter, you can cut a doorway, using the same energy employed for opening the circle. Using your right hand, starting at the floor, slice up, over, and down again, through the circle wall, forming a rectangle large enough to pass through. Picture the energy of the circle shimmering and sparking all around the doorway, but holding firm; I envision something out of a sci-fi movie, a portal to another dimension, with tendrils of light swirling at the edges like spiderwebs caught in a summer wind. When you return to the circle, and all is well again, simply close the door by drawing the rectangle in reverse; the wall of light smoothes and stills behind you, with nary a ripple.

# seven

# ELEMENTAL MAGIC: WORKING WITH VARIOUS ENERGIES

*Be still, wild music is abroad.*

—Henry Wadsworth Longfellow

There are many layers to magic in the Craft, many different sources from which spiritual and mystical influence emanate. These sources are known as "correspondences," things and ideas that correspond to the magical work at hand. The alchemy of a spell requires that as many of the correspondences as possible work together to ensure the greatest energetic synthesis to support your magical purpose.

Just as there are specific influences in the phases of the Moon, so too are there particular magical qualities inherent in colors, planets, crystals, the days of the week, the four directions, and the elements of earth, air, fire, and water.

Following are several tables of correspondences. Think of them as lists of magical ingredients that when mixed concoct the necessary power and intent to bring your spells to fruition.

## DAYS OF THE WEEK

### Sunday

*Magical Intent:* Health or Healing, Success, Prosperity, Creativity, Confidence, Hope, Physical Strength

    *Element:* Fire

    *Planet:* The Sun

    *Astrological Sign:* Leo

    *Colors:* Gold, Orange, Yellow

    *Herbs:* Chamomile, Cloves, Frankincense, Ambergris, Sunflower, Heliotrope, Cedar

    *Crystals:* Carnelian, Amber, Topaz, Citrine

### Monday

*Magical Intent:* Psychic Development, Dream Work, Intuition, Visions, Emotional Balance, Women's Mysteries, Karma, Reincarnation, Home and Hearth, Beauty

    *Element:* Water

    *Planet:* The Moon

    *Astrological Sign:* Cancer

*Colors:* White, Silver, Pearl, Pale Pink, Lavender

*Herbs:* White Rose and Poppy, Night-Blooming Jasmine, Willow, Myrtle, Moonwort, Camphor, Vervain

*Crystals:* Moonstone, Pearl, Quartz Crystal, Fluorite, Selenite, Aquamarine

## Tuesday

*Magical Intent:* Passion, Courage, Destiny, Goals, Strength, Action, Kundalini, Sexuality, Swift Movement, Energy

*Elements:* Fire, Water

*Planet:* Mars

*Astrological Signs:* Aries, Scorpio

*Color:* Red

*Herbs:* Carnation, Patchouli, Red Rose, Pepper, Garlic, Nettle, Cactus, Pine

*Crystals:* Bloodstone, Ruby, Garnet, Carnelian, Hematite, Pink Tourmaline

## Wednesday

*Magical Intent:* Communication, Writing, Education, Public Speaking, Wisdom, Intellect, Motivation, Prediction, Memory

*Element:* Earth

*Planets:* Mercury, Chiron

*Astrological Sign:* Virgo

*Colors:* Orange, Green, Yellow, Light Blue, Gray

*Herbs:* Lavender, Sweetpea, Cinnamon, Dill, Cinquefoil, Fern, Periwinkle, Hazel

*Crystals:* Opal, Aventurine, Sodalite, Moss Agate, Bloodstone

## Thursday

*Magical Intent:* Legal Matters, Business, Politics, Employment, Bartering, Honors, Good Fortune, Logic, Material and Financial Wealth

*Elements:* Fire, Water

*Planet:* Jupiter

*Astrological Signs:* Sagittarius, Pisces

*Colors:* Purple, Royal Blue, Turquoise

*Herbs:* Lilac, Nutmeg, Cinnamon, Coltsfoot, Saffron, Cedar, Oak, Pine

*Crystals:* Amethyst, Turquoise, Lapis Lazuli, Sugilite, Sapphire

## Friday

*Magical Intent:* Love, Friendship, Partnerships, Fertility, Sensuality, Money, Artistic Pursuits, Harmony, New Projects, Beauty, Soulmates

*Elements:* Earth, Air

*Planet:* Venus

*Astrological Signs:* Libra, Taurus

*Colors:* Pink, Green, Pale Green, Sky Blue

*Herbs:* Verbena, Pink Rose, Ivy, Apple Blossom, Violet, Lily, Sage, Yarrow, Birch

*Crystals:* Rose Quartz, Pink Tourmaline, Emerald, Jade, Peridot, Malachite

## Saturday

*Magical Intent:* Protection, Neutralization, Binding, Manifestation, Discipline, Family, Duty, Completion

*Elements:* Earth, Air, Fire, Water

*Planet:* Saturn

*Astrological Signs:* Capricorn, Aquarius

*Colors:* Black, Navy Blue, Brown

*Herbs:* Nightshade, Mandrake, Rue, Wolfsbane, Moss, Myrrh, Ivy, Hemlock, Black Poppy, Oak

*Crystals:* Obsidian, Black Onyx, Diamond, Jet, Smoky Quartz, Amethyst, Garnet

So, how do you use these magical elements?

Say a spell for financial prosperity is called for. First you would check the phase of the Moon, detailed in chapter 5.

Then, since Thursday is the day of the week that corresponds with material and financial wealth, you would choose a Thursday during either the Waxing or Full Moon phase. Using the other correspondences for Thursday, you might incorporate a purple or royal blue altar cloth, or wear either of those colors and perhaps some turquoise jewelry. Use oak leaves, cinnamon sticks, or lilacs to decorate the altar, and a big African amethyst or a lapis sphere. Fire and water are the appropriate elements, so any of the deities such as Brigid, who represents both, or Aidan, an Irish God of fire, can be invoked to add their special energies.

But let's imagine for a moment that you've checked your calendar, and there is no way on the Goddess' green Earth that you'll be able to do a ritual on that perfect Thursday. Does this mean you must wait until next month, even though the bills are piling up and the checking account is thinning? Of course not! Remember, in Witchcraft, there is always more than one way to pet a cat...

## THE FOUR DIRECTIONS

### North

*Magical Intent:* Manifestation, Fertility, Physical Strength, Health, Wealth, Property, Tangible Success

*Element:* Earth

*Season:* Winter

*Colors:* Green, Brown

*Animals:* Wolf, Elk, Bear

*Tarot Suit:* Pentacles

## South

*Magical Intent:* Creativity, Passion, Spirituality, Sexuality, Ambition, Courage

*Element:* Fire

*Season:* Summer

*Colors:* Red, Gold

*Animals:* Lizard, Snake, Lion

*Tarot Suit:* Wands

## East

*Magical Intent:* Wisdom, Intellect, Communication, Legal Matters

*Element:* Air

*Season:* Spring

*Colors:* Pink, Yellow

*Animals:* Eagle, Raven, Hawk

*Tarot Suit:* Swords

**West**

*Magical Intent:* Psychic Development, Dream Work, Emotional Balance, Creativity, Love, Joy

    *Element:* Water

    *Season:* Autumn

    *Colors:* Blue, Lavender

    *Animals:* Dolphin, Swan, Whale

    *Tarot Suit:* Cups

To work with directions instead of days, take that same prosperity spell, choose whatever day works for you within either the Waxing or Full Moon phases, and set up your altar facing North, which is the direction for wealth and manifestation. Dress in green or brown, or use the colors ornamentally; call in the animal energies of a great mother bear or a wise old wolf to assist you in your work. Have crystals, stones, salt, and a potted plant on hand to represent the element of earth, and use Tarot cards from the suit of Pentacles as visual focus; the Ace, for instance, denotes the beginning of financial gain, while the Nine depicts material abundance and luxury and the Ten means financial security and lasting wealth. Same spell, different day, just as powerful.

    Okay, you say. Fabulous. But what if the wolf, rather than wise and supportive, is salivating at your door, the Moon's in a Waning phase, and you haven't got a minute to spare . . . I say, slow down! Besides needing the correct combination of earthly elements, a spell requires a certain calm, an attitude of deliberation and intent, in order for the magic to work. A huge part of successful spellwork is trusting that the God and Goddess are *always* protecting and guiding you, magic or no. But for the sake of those moments in life that require quick and decisive action, there is a simple recipe for immediate magical assistance ...

## COLOR MAGIC

**Red:** Love, Lust, Passion, Attraction, Strength, Courage, Life Force, Career Goals, Survival Issues, First Chakra

**Pink:** Romance, Friendship, Nurturing, Motherhood, Emotional Healing, Peace

**Orange:** Energy, Ambition, Legal Matters, Sales, Property Deals, Business Goals, Second Chakra

**Yellow:** The Sun, Confidence, Persuasion, Memory, Intellect, Education, Creativity, Third Chakra

**Green:** Money, Health, Growth, Fertility, Earth and Plant Magic, Personal Goals, Fourth Chakra

**Blue:** Inspiration, Wisdom, Astral Projection, Spiritual Growth, Peace, Prophecy, Fifth and Sixth Chakras

**Purple:** Protection, Psychic Ability, Spiritual Power, Success, Influence, Healing, Seventh Chakra

**Black:** Protection, Binding, Banishing

**White:** Spirituality, Purity, Peace, Meditation, Divination, Truth, The Goddess (white is also a substitute for all other colors)

**Silver:** The Goddess, Communication, Intuition, Dreams, Astral Travel, Feminine Power

**Gold:** The God, Wealth, Winning, Happiness, Playfulness, Masculine Power

Color magic is one of the simplest yet most effective methods around. You can use color magically in myriad ways. Clothing is one of the easiest. For instance, if you're going to the bank to ask for a loan to start your own business, you might wear yellow for confidence and persuasion, green for money, purple for success, or orange for ambition and business goals.

Carrying stones, scraps of paper or fabric, or charm bags (small cloth bags filled with magically charged herbs, crystals, and the like) of corresponding colors is another easy method. Ink on paper is a great little conjuring; write your need or desire on a small piece of appropriately colored parchment in a corresponding ink, roll it up in a little scroll, and either burn it as an offering to the Goddess or tuck it away on your altar or somewhere sacred until it manifests.

Color can be used in healing the body, particularly in working with the chakra system or acupressure points. And sometimes simply "seeing" a color in your mind's eye, or meditating upon it, is magic enough to get the proverbial ball rolling. ("Seeing red" when you're angry? Not just a metaphor. Anger is simply passion, misdirected. Next time visualize blue or white, or "cool" your anger into a soothing Jordan Almond pink.)

One of the best uses of color magic is with candles. Dressing and burning a magically charged candle is powerful, and the results are often immediate (details in chapter 6).

So let's take our previous spell, forgoing the Full Moon in the North on Thursday (but only for the sake of demonstration!), and have you light a perfect little green candle that, despite your hurry, has been properly dressed and now smells like it belongs on top of a warm slice of apple pie (remember the cinnamon oil for prosperity!). Gazing at the dancing flame, speak your words of need to the Goddess, humbly, thankfully, knowing full well that she's not only listening but likely putting things into motion even as you speak.

You can add spice to this spell, figuratively, by incorporating the ink and paper scroll mentioned earlier (this time fold the paper and place it under the candleholder, then burn it or keep it on your altar), and literally, by sprinkling powdered cinnamon onto the candle flame. It creates the most wonderful little shower of magical sparks and adds yet another layer of intent to your work. Let the candle burn out by itself or, if you must, snuff the flame, leave the candle undisturbed on your altar, and light it again when you can, as often as necessary, until it is gone. Some candle spells are written for specific performance over a period of days, such as an attraction spell in which the candle is burned every night from the New Moon to the Full. For a good all-purpose candle spell, see chapter 10.

## CASTING A SPELL

In a perfect world, with perfect timing, and with all the correspondences perfectly in place, what might a prosperity spell look like? Picture this:

On a Thursday night just prior to the Full Moon, dressed in a cerulean robe trimmed with purple, wearing an amethyst pendant and your grandmother's sapphire ring, you set your altar facing magnetic North, and drape it in blue or green satin. Gold and silver candlesticks honor the God and Goddess, and evoke the countenance of wealth. You arrange lilacs, oak leaves, and a few sprays of cedar in a gleaming brass bowl. Dollar bills and a string of turquoise or malachite beads lie among your ritual tools. A dish of salt and a carved Zuni fetish of a bear sit beside the Ten of Pentacles from the Robin Wood Tarot deck, and the sweet smoke of cloves and nutmeg fills the air.

A handful of coins glitters at the base of a green pillar candle, set upon the Pentacle at the center of your altar; the candle wax smells of patchouli and spice, and is carved with dollar signs, prosperity runes, and the astrological symbol for Jupiter. You cast the circle, invoke the God and Goddess, and invite your favorite fire and fertility deities to join the party. You light the candle, read your words of power from a mint-green parchment scroll written in metallic gold ink, all the while visualizing yourself surrounded by riches.

Ritual should evoke a shift in consciousness, stirring up a strong emotional response to your desires and creating an experiential connection to absolute possibility. The more corresponding elements you can put together in a ritual, the more of an emotional environment will result. The above scenario was for the sake of illustrating ambience, but as we've discussed previously, magic doesn't have to be fancy to be effective.

And remember, magic is not a quick fix to escape your problems. In fact, if you are having self-created money challenges and you perform a spell for prosperity, you'll likely conjure some interesting opportunities to learn how to handle your finances constructively first.

Every spell I have ever cast has manifested. Not always in my preferred timeframe (which to an impatient Sagittarian is a lesson in and of itself), and not always as I had pictured them, but come to fruition they have, with miraculous results. If a spell does *not* work, it's usually due to wording, lack of focus, or vague intent. But in the Craft, you come to heed well the adage

"Be Careful What You Wish For"—you're likely to get it, and then some!

Magic invokes Divine assistance *for the highest good of all concerned.* Sometimes what can seem a failure is simply your good being rerouted. So trust is perhaps *the* essential element to have in place before you cast your circle.

Of all the correspondences, the most important are the phases of the Moon. Then come the combinations of the elements, the directions, and color. Work with what you have, substitute what works, and trust that the God and Goddess are already one step ahead of you, anticipating your needs and your intent.

Magic is an alignment with universal laws and energies to effect needed or desired change. The trimmings, the trappings, the colors, and the symbols are only to align *you* with the magic. Spirit doesn't need us to pray. Spirit doesn't need us to cast circles, burn green candles, or drum and dance in the moonlight. *We* need to do these things. The God and Goddess can only do for us what they can do through us, and they can only do through us if we are all on the same page, so to speak. Ritual and ceremony are how we connect our mind and emotions to our spirit, bridging the gap between the human and the Divine. Aligning with the elements means aligning with the gods in tangible, *earthly* ways.

Wicca isn't all candles and chants; it is also tuning in to the synchronicity and symbology of our lives, and learning to speak the language of both Heaven and Earth. To walk in the world with awareness; to create, consciously; to partner with one's own God; and to recognize, welcome, and work miracles ... this is what it means to be a Witch, and this is the true stuff of magic.

# eight

# WORDS OF POWER
# AND THE POWER OF WORDS:
# CREATING SPELLS

*Sticks and stones may break my bones,*
*but words can never hurt me.*

—English proverb

Ever since I was a child, I've thought that the above saying was totally absurd. In literal terms (and the psychological effects of physical abuse notwithstanding), bruises do fade, flesh and bone recreate themselves, but words and ideas can be carried, unchanged, for a lifetime. Our words, our language, set up a physical, vibrational force in the ethers; as human beings, we are constantly creating our reality from that force, either by the words we speak aloud or by the constant commentaries we run inside our own minds.

As a writer, teacher, and spiritual counselor, I know full well the power of words. As a Neuro-Linguistic Programming (NLP) practitioner, I work with clients on a daily basis to change the "language of the brain," to erase the negative tapes of childhood and create a new, positive, affirming inner dialogue. I see people whose entire identities have been molded from criticism given them decades ago. I also see those same people completely change their lives by refusing the judgments and learning to claim themselves worthy.

Words, and the energy they produce, have absolute power to heal or destroy. In the Craft, we believe a Witch's word *is* his or her power. And the process of creating spells and rituals for magic elevates language to a truly sacred art.

## WHAT IS A SPELL?

A spell is a combination of specific words, emotional expression, and mental projection. More simply put, a spell is a prayer "acted out"; the magic circle is the stage, your magical tools are the props, and your will and intent are the range of emotion you employ to ensure an award-winning performance.

There are countless variations of spells employing different "magical catalysts" or ingredients, such as candle spells, spells using knotted cords, "poppet" spells using handmade dolls, kitchen or food spells, and spells using containers such as boxes, jars, bags, or envelopes. There is literally no end to the creative methods Witches come up with to establish magical intent.

Spells are best written out, the words and phrasing considered with the utmost care. I have been known to take days to formulate a particular spell, as I have learned the hard way about impeccability, or the lack thereof, in anything pertaining to magic. At the very least, a poorly planned spell will simply fizzle out; in the worst-case scenario, it can blow up in your face.

There are plenty of stories about spells gone awry due to careless composition. Spells for money "to pay all the bills" can result in an avalanche of old debts surfacing, demanding full and immediate remittance plus interest. A far more extreme example is casting a spell asking for a specific and substantial amount of cash; it indeed manifests, but in the form of an insurance settlement from an auto accident that leaves you paralyzed. A better way to word money spells? Ask for "more than enough money and resources for all personal needs, desires, and obligations," and affirm that said resources come "easily and joyfully" or "quickly, easily, and in peace."

Spells should be composed with as much detail as possible. For instance, asking the gods for "the perfect relationship" might result in conjuring the perfect opportunity for experiencing firsthand all the things you *don't* want in a relationship! You can still ask for "perfect," but flesh that out with statements such as the person being "healthy in mind, body, and spirit," "kind and generous," and the all-important "Single and Available." As inspirational writer and minister Catherine Ponder says, "Get definite about your desires so they can get definite about you!"

Some Witches rhyme their spells. Rhyming spells are fun, easy to remember, and create a great rhythm for movement and energy building. My working rituals always contain a rhyme or two, but the main body of my spells, which I call the "statement of intent," are composed as deliberate, affirmative declarations. These are my "words of power," specific in objective but open regarding the outcome they create.

For example, if I were in need of a new computer, I would prepare a statement of intent using these or similar words:

> *"O Gracious Goddess, O Gracious God, know my*
> *need and hear my prayer. I ask for your assistance*
> *in finding and purchasing the perfect computer for*
> *my professional and personal use. This computer*
> *is of the highest quality, is in excellent working*
> *order, and is offered to me at the perfect price.*
> *This computer comes to me quickly, easily, and in*
> *peace, and I am completely satisfied and happy*
> *with the outcome."*

If I had a specific brand in mind, or even a particular model number I really wanted, I would state it, but add, "or something better" as a fail-safe, just in case the gods are more computer savvy than I am (I'm being facetious. The gods are *always* more savvy than us, about everything; in this case, where computers and me are concerned, my *dog* is more savvy.) Remember that naming the form your desire takes can limit it. Be willing to turn the outcome of your spell over to the God and Goddess, and be open for the very best.

You can also add statements regarding specific timelines if you want, such as "I ask that this come forth for me within the next three weeks, six months, etc." If you perform a spell during an Esbat, it's customary to ask for fulfillment by the time the Moon comes round to Full again. However, you want to be very flexible, affirming "Divine timing for the good of all concerned."

Now, if money was an obstacle for me regarding this desire, I might revise my statement of intent to read "I ask your assistance in drawing to me the perfect computer, which manifests for me now in Divine ways," leaving out the bit about the perfect price. That way I leave the door open for the computer to be a gift, or a contest prize, as opposed to a purchase. Or, I could add a phrase such as "I have more than enough money for this purchase, and the money comes to me quickly, easily, and in peace, through the rich avenues of Divine substance." This would hold the space for the money to be gifted to me or for a wonderful windfall to manifest.

Next, I would add what I call my "accident" or "escape" clauses—all-purpose statements that help to cover the proverbial bases. Choose among them or, when in doubt, play it safe and use them all.

> *"I ask the universe to lend the power of the planets*
> *in their orbits, the stars in their courses, the*

*angels, and the elements of earth, air, fire, and
water, all to blend in perfect order and harmony,
to obtain my desire."*

(This statement adds a little extra cosmic oomph, and is very useful when performing a spell during an incorrect Moon phase or when you're lacking a good dose of magical correspondences.)

*"Anything I may have overlooked in this spell will
be taken care of for me with perfect, Divine
results, in the God's (or the Goddess') own perfect
way."*

(Excellent for dispelling that "I feel like I've forgotten something" sensation.)

*"This or something better now comes forth for me,
in perfect timing, for the highest good of all concerned."*

(This one's particularly crucial, in my opinion. As stated earlier, human beings are limited by nature; Spirit is all-seeing, and it's important to let the God and Goddess know you're flexible, and that you gladly accept upgrades.)

Finally, as a wrap-up, I would write the following statement:

*"I give thanks for the perfect, Divine results now!
So Mote It Be!"*

After composing my words of power (usually a process involving lots of notebook paper, writing and rewriting until I'm completely satisfied), I copy them carefully onto magically charged parchment paper with consecrated ink, making a "magical scroll" that I can incorporate into a working ritual.

I then gather up any visual aids or symbolic items that I might want to have on my altar when I perform the spell. If I have a picture of a computer from a magazine ad, or perhaps a brochure of the exact one I covet, I would use it to help focus my intent. If necessary, I could draw a picture; you don't have to be an artist to do this, even the crudest hieroglyphic figure on paper is powerful. This is known as "sympathetic magic," or imaging, using pictures or symbols of an object to draw it to you, like the cave paintings of our earliest ancestors.

Take your time when crafting your spells. Truly think about what you want to create in your life; ask yourself pertinent questions about the motivation behind your desire. For example, If I get this, what will it do for me? Get clear about the essence of the thing you want, and leave the outcome in the hands of Spirit. Affirm your efforts are working *for the highest good of all concerned.*

It is said that the sung or spoken word is at least 80 percent more powerful than prayers said in silence. Some cultures believe that the moment you speak a thing, you claim it, and so become it. In Witchcraft, spells are whispered, chanted, sung, or even shouted (joyfully, of course!) to the heavens, in the complete confidence that they shall indeed be heard, and that the vibrations created by our words will set in motion all that is necessary to bring our desires into being.

# nine

# THE STRUCTURE OF RITUAL

*Once upon a time, in a land far, far away...*

—Opening line of any self-respecting fairy-tale

Performing ritual is much like telling a story. There is a natural flow, a rhythm and design that is powerful, instinctual, and essential to myth. First, the opening, which sets the mood and pulls you immediately into the landscape of the tale; the introduction of the heroes and heroines for whom the adventure unfolds; the heart of the journey, and the spirit of the quest; the climax, where the pinnacle is reached and the victory is won; and finally the ending, in which, of course, everyone lives happily ever after.

I'm going to walk you through the storyline of ritual to give you the lay of the land, so to speak. Once again, we're treading wide-open spaces here; there are many, many ways to do ritual, and this is only one. I'll lead you through the motions, like staging a play: I'll show you your marks and we'll talk about focus and intent, but we'll save the actual script (the words and ritual incantations) for chapter 10.

In Wicca, there are two types of ritual: celebratory and working. Celebratory rituals include those of the Sabbats as well as rites of passage such as handfastings (marriages), namings (christenings), and coming-of-age ceremonies; working rituals are performed at the Esbats, or any time spells or magical endeavors are needed or desired. Following are descriptions of the most common working rituals:

**Initiations:** A combination of both celebratory and working ritual, wherein the Witch dedicates himself or herself to the Craft and the path of the Goddess. These rituals can be quite formal (in some covens they follow an apprenticeship of a year and a day), or they can be simple self-dedication rites performed by a solitary at the beginning of his or her path, and can include the consecration of ritual tools.

**Banishing:** Also known as a cleansing, banishings remove old, unwanted energy from a person, place, or thing, usually by employing the four elements with salt, water, fire, and smoke. This ritual is used for such things as clearing magical tools, ritual objects, houses, or cars, or to remove blocks, obstacles, or challenges you might be experiencing in creating your desires.

**Blessing:** A blessing generally follows a banishing. This ritual is designed to instill the power and protection of the God and Goddess once the unwanted energy is gone.

**Attraction:** Attraction magic is worked to help magnetize or bring to you the thing or experience you desire, such as money, love, right livelihood, etc.

**Healing:** A healing is a specific combination of cleansing and blessing for the benefit of someone who is ailing. These can be tricky, and absolutely require the permission of the recipient. Conditions can worsen before they get better, as the body and mind have their own unique order of process, and caution must be exercised. If permission for a direct healing is impossible to obtain, the energy can instead be sent into the ethers for the recipient to employ on his or her own, either consciously or through Divine intervention. Healings can be performed on animals as well, but the same rules apply; obtain permission from the owner, or send the energy into the cosmos for the God and Goddess to dispense.

**Protection:** Protection magic can be performed to neutralize, dispel, or deflect negative energy. Binding spells can also be performed to protect you from a difficult or dangerous person, but these must be done with absolute consciousness, being extremely careful to abide by the law "Harm None."

**Divination:** A specific magic ritual to aid in the use of divinatory tools such as the Tarot, pendulums, scrying mirrors, or astrological charts. Using these tools ritually in sacred space can help minimize distraction and tap you into a deeper level of psychic and intuitive information.

Before a ritual begins, all the essential elements must be in place. The spell you're planning to work should be well thought out, carefully worded, constructed with all the appropriate correspondences, and all the magical supplies you'll need should be in hand. Once the stage is set, the tale is ripe for the telling.

*It was a dark and stormy night...*

—Opening line of any self-respecting mystery novel

Here's where we set the mood. Ritual can be performed at any time of the day or night; in fact, timing involves a whole other set of correspondences—the numerological and astrological aspects of the hours (check an almanac or numerology book for more details). I prefer to do my magical work in the flickering candlelight, either at 9 P.M., the hour of the Goddess, or at midnight, the hour of the Witch.

The landscape of your ritual is, of course, the magic circle. But first, there are some ways to purify and ready the ritual space and yourself, to prepare the atmosphere and to align the environment energetically to your purpose. A cast circle in and of itself is a purification of both space and person, but the following measures will only add to your magic, and shouldn't be missed if at all possible.

**Preparation of Self:** This step should definitely be followed, at least to some degree, to ensure the proper emotional energy and frame of mind for meeting the deities, and for working magic. Start with a ritual bath or shower; sea salt is a sacred cleansing tool, and aromatherapy products can be used to induce a state of peace and well-being. Wash off the cares of the day; visualize releasing any tension or worry into the perfumed water, and let it be drained away.

It's important to come into the circle clear, focused, and, for lack of a better descriptive, in a good mood. Whatever energy you bring into ritual gets expanded; energy raised is a force all its own. Early on in my practice I had one bad experience (it only took one!) where I cast a circle when I was feeling very anxious and frustrated, without bothering to calm myself down first. It took me a week to clear the tension from the air in my apartment, and to feel as though I could stay in my own skin.

If a shower or bath can't be on the agenda, other ways to cleanse yourself of unwanted energy include meditation, yoga, drumming, chanting, deep breathing, or smudging, a Native American ritual of burning white sage with other purifying herbs and fanning the spicy smoke across your body. Pick at least one, and use it to consciously shed the skin of the day before you cross that magical threshold.

Dress for ritual is purely personal. Some Witches practice their magic "skyclad," a poetic Wiccan term for "in the buff." Robes are another option; choose a color that has magical meaning for you, and choose a style that is comfortable and nonconstricting, but without a lot of excess fabric, particularly in the sleeves. (While billowing sleeves might indeed add to the pageantry of your ritual, flaming sleeves would not!) Special, consecrated jewelry can be worn, and shoes if you desire. I prefer to feel the ground (albeit the floor, most of the time) directly against the soles of my bare feet.

**Preparation of Space:** Clean the floor physically: vacuum, sweep with a household broom, or mop. When I lived in a house with hardwood floors, I would steep dried lavender and rosemary in boiling water, then mop and wash down the walls. Lavender and rosemary are purifying herbs, and the smell they create is intoxicating!

Next, energetically "sweep," this time with your ritual broom. (Only *after* you've consecrated it! Skip this step until then.) The broom needn't actually touch the ground; visualize the same kind of effervescent light with which you cast your circle sparking from the bristles, clearing away every last shadow.

Sprinkling salt or saltwater, drumming, or purifying with incense or smudge are other ways to energetically prepare the ritual space. Walk the perimeter of the circle, visualizing the herbs or the salt or the music dissolving away any negative or static energy. Picture the floor, the atmosphere, as crystalline as a mountain pool, ready for you and your magical work.

Next, set up the altar in the center of your clean space. Some

Traditions specify that the altar face North, the direction of strength and manifestation. Others say East, the direction of wisdom and communication. In my rituals, the altar faces South, which is my astrological direction—the element of fire, creativity, spirituality, passion. The bottom line here? Place your altar facing in whichever direction feels right to you. Experiment. Try a different direction each time, and observe the energy that is created, or choose the direction that corresponds to the intent of your magic.

Make sure you have everything you will need to perform your rite on or near the altar; it's easy to forget the lighter for the candles, or the cord for the Knot Spell, and then have to interrupt your ritual to leave the circle.

Along with your other magical tools, make sure you have a stick of incense (chosen for appropriate fragrance), a small red candle in a holder, a chalice filled with water (use a cup or bowl if the chalice is not yet consecrated), and a dish of salt. These will represent the four elements, and with them you will consecrate the altar (declare it sacred in the name of the God and Goddess or your chosen deities) to begin the ritual. Also, be sure to have an appropriately colored candle to represent the God, and one for the Goddess, at the head of the altar, as described in chapter 6.

Now, take a few moments to relax, breathe deeply, and let your mind turn toward magic. Be fully present in the ritual space. It's time to begin.

**I. Creating Sacred Space:** Consecrating the altar consists of lighting the incense and the red candle, then sprinkling the water and then the salt (sparingly) in a clockwise circle, all the while picturing the elements purifying the altar and everything on it. The red candle is the first flame to be lit, and the effect is quite enchanting in the darkness. Imagine presenting the elements as offerings, and your altar as a gift to the gods. Do this, as everything, with intent.

Then, when you are ready, cast your circle.

**II. Invocation:** Enter the hero and heroine; enter the champions to our cause, the elements of nature and the four directions. This part of ritual, when the deities and the elements are called to join the circle, is known as the *invocation*.

First, standing at the altar, invoke the God and the Goddess as you envision them. As you light their candles and speak the words of welcome, picture them stepping into the circle (wild and beautiful), smiling at you in the half-lit darkness. You *feel* them—their power, their kindness, their pleasure in your company. Let yourself believe, and experience this; it is a spine-tingling, extraordinary moment.

Next, either facing the four directions where you stand or going to the edge of the circle in the North, East, South, and West, invoke the spirits of earth, air, fire, and water, respectively. Notice that you move clockwise around the circle, the same way in which you cast it; take your time at each station. Picture totem animals, warriors, angels, energy beings, or anything else your heart and imagination might desire. See them moving into the candlelight; sense the presence and mood of these powerful spirits, feeling their protection all around you.

After the elements are called, for a moment stand quietly at the altar to proclaim the sacred space. Be present with all who have joined you, and let yourself revel in the magic.

> *Here between the worlds am I,*
> *child of Earth and child of Sky...*
>
> —Traditional

**III. The Body of the Ritual:** Next comes the heart of the working ritual, when the quest is taken up and the journey begins. It is time to entreat the gods, speak your words of power, cast your spells, and work your miracles. This is also the point in a Sabbat ritual when you would observe the sacred rite of that holiday. Specific deities can be invoked now for magical workings; in an Esbat, you would draw down the Moon and cast whatever spell you've chosen to perform, embodying the Goddess' shimmering light.

At this point in ritual, intent and concentration are key. This is where your powers of visualization are put to the test, and you build the energy necessary to release your desire to the Universe. As you read from your magical scroll, carve your candles, mix your herbs, or speak your words of power, picture the results into being; see them in your mind's eye, form them in the air before you. Taste your words. Work with deliberation; speak boldly, and with purpose.

When you have finished stating your intent and your magical task is complete, spend a moment focusing your energy upon it. If you've incorporated any visual aids in your spell, use them now to see yourself with the object of your desire, to picture yourself in the experience. Take your time with this. Feel what it will be like when your desire is manifest. Don't be afraid of detail here. Daydream; trust your imagination as an unsurpassed and unlimited tool for creating reality, and turn it loose in the sanctity of the circle.

**IV: Raising and Releasing the Energy:** This is the climax of our story—the hero and heroine, racing for the top of the mountain, their victory at hand; here's where you charge your desire with magical rocket fuel, sending it straight to the heavens.

Still focusing on your intent, still picturing your desire coming into being, begin to move about the circle. Physically engage with the energy you're creating: dance, sway, move in any manner that moves you. Be sure to head clockwise around the circle (*deosil* for raising, *widdershins* for banishing), taking care not to bump the altar or snag a stray hem on a candle flame. Rhyming chants are perfect here, as are drums, rattles, bells, tambourines, or any other rhythmic instrument; you can simply sing or chant the essence of your desire over and over again as you move.

Begin to move faster. The air within the circle is warm, and spiced with the incense; it grows warmer by the minute. The energy of your voice, your vision, begins to spiral up and up. Faster. The energy is building, growing in you and within the circle like some mythic creature rising up through a mist. *Faster.* The circle glows around you; you chant louder, and louder; the drum slams out the rhythm of your heart, your body flushes with the fire of your purpose, and just before it reaches its peak, you stop, throw your hands into the air, and release the energy into the atmosphere, the culmination of your magic streaming from your fingertips like a thousand stars going nova in the darkness.

Breathe. Ground what is left, placing your hands against the floor. Let whatever power remains sink into and restore Mother Earth.

It is finished.

**V. Opening the Circle:** Now comes the part where the hero and heroine ride off together into the sunset, and the champions return to their homeland, victorious.

After you've grounded the energy of your spell, it's time to ground your physical body and celebrate with the magical feast or, as it's traditionally known, "Cakes and Ale," a simple snack of cookies, bread, cheese, or traditional crescent-shaped cakes served with juice, wine, or water. This blessing and ritual imbibing of food and drink helps to bring the body back down to earth from spiritual rapture. (Have the food on or near the altar before the ritual begins.)

Hold the food up in salute and say the blessing; do the same for the drink. As you eat, imagine the God and Goddess partaking with you in the ageless and sacred ritual of breaking bread. You can have a special dish or libation bowl on the altar in which to place a bit of the food, then pour this onto the ground outside as an offering after the ritual.

*Relax.* Let yourself mentally and physically "come back" into the ritual space; walk about, sit, or, as I've been known to do more than once, lie down and let your mind consort with miracles. You feel calm, strengthened, vitalized; the magic you worked still whispers at the edge of the circle. Stay as long as you like in this charmed place.

Finally, it is time to bid farewell to the spirits and the powers that presided over your rite. Begin again in the North, then move counterclockwise along the circle to the West, South, and East, thanking the spirits of the four elements for their protection. See them turn and move away into the darkness beyond; know that they will come again gladly whenever you ask.

Standing once more at the altar, spend a few final moments with your Lord and Lady, giving thanks for all their blessings. As they disappear into the shadows, be comforted by the knowledge that they are always beside you, and any time you cast a circle, they will be there. You snuff their candles, first silver, than gold; the ritual space falls into a blessed darkness. And in the flickering light of the first and now the last ritual flame, you part the circle; the air cools, the curtain of magic falls away, and all is done.

There is no "right" amount of time to spend in any part of the ritual. Concentrate for as long as you can on whatever you are doing; when you feel your attention waver or you start to get physically or mentally tired, it's time to move on to the next step. This could be a minute, or an hour. As with all things in the Craft, *trust the magic, and yourself.* All is unfolding exactly as it should.

# ten

# THE RITES

*Shall we write about the things not to be spoken of? Shall we divulge the things not to be divulged? Shall we pronounce the things not to be pronounced?*

—The Magical Papyri

In this chapter, you'll find the "script" for the ritual we walked through in chapter 9, as well as a rite of consecration, self-dedication, a Full Moon ceremony, and two basic spells to get you started. The text is set up so that you can insert any of the rites or spells beginning on page 133, or any of your own finds or creations, into part III of the basic ritual on page 127.

I vividly remember my first ritual. The altar was an absolute work of art, the Moon was smiling down on me through the living room window, my dress shimmered softly in the candle-light, even my bare toes were freshly polished. And there I was, trying to balance a book in one hand and do my magic with the other, dreadfully concerned lest I forget my lines or, Goddess forbid, walk counter when I meant to go clockwise. It was still a divine experience, but more awkward than I ever anticipated. Then I got smart, and for awhile, my altar was peppered with little "cheat sheets," small pieces of parchment (consecrated, of course!) upon which I had written the various invocations and ritual rhymes. It took the pressure off, allowing me to get comfortable with the intrigues of ceremony, to truly *feel* what I was creating without worrying about doing it perfectly.

Familiarize yourself with the ritual structure in chapter 9. Get comfortable with the order of things, the mood, and the movements. The emotional aspect of ritual is far more important than the intellectual; learn the expressions first, and then, if it comes easy to you, memorize the invocations. If not, write them down. You'll know them by heart soon enough. You aren't going to be critiqued by some great cosmic director on whether or not you deliver your lines without error on opening night. But you might walk away thinking "Is that all there is?" if you aren't engaged in the energy of what you're doing. Ritual is first and foremost a spiritual experience; the pageantry is a secondary delight.

And another thing—know that the gods have a terrific sense of humor. They won't be keeping score if you light the wrong candle, spill the Holy Water, or invoke the spirits of the East when you're standing in the West. If you screw up, start over, and have yourself a good giggle in the process. Laughter creates a magic all its own.

Practice walking the circle and welcoming the gods. Then

take the words on the following pages and speak them by rote, change them, or throw them out and write your own. Witchcraft is an art, and in this class, you don't have to color inside the lines unless you want to.

## A SIMPLE RITUAL

**Supplies:**

Incense

One small red candle in a holder

Bowl or chalice of water

Dish of salt

Candles to represent the God and Goddess

Cakes and Ale

Lighter

Your ritual tools, and all supplies required for whatever spell or rite you are performing

### I. Creating Sacred Space

Consecration of the altar:

*"Inspired with air."* (Light incense.)

*"Enlightened with fire."* (Light red candle.)

*"Cleansed with water."* (Sprinkle water.)

*"Strengthened with earth."* (Sprinkle salt.)

*"Infused with Spirit."* (Hold hands over center of altar in blessing.)

> *"In the name of the Goddess, Enchantress, and Queen, and of the God, her consort and King, I hereby consecrate this altar. May it serve in their honor as the seat of wisdom and the heart of magic. So Mote It Be!"*

Cast the circle, using your wand, athame, or your right hand.

> *"I cast this circle, once around,*
> *All within by magic bound.*
> *A sacred space, a healing place,*
> *Safe from harm by Spirit's grace."*

## II. Invocation

Stand at the altar.

Invoke the Goddess:

> *"Wondrous Lady of the Moon,*
> *Mistress of Magic and Mother of all,*
> *I welcome you to my circle this night.*
> *Bless this space with your light and your love."*

Light the Goddess candle.

>*"The Lady is come, and welcome!"*

Invoke the God:

>*"Radiant Lord of the Sun,*
>    *Master of beasts wild and free; protector*
>    *of all,*
>*I welcome you to my circle this night.*
>*Bless this space with your light and your*
>    *love."*

Light the God candle.

>*"The Lord is come, and welcome!"*

Invoke the four directions:

>*"Spirits of the North,*
>    *Powers of earth,*
>    *Come and be present in my circle.*
>    *Bless me with your strength, and your*
>        *faith.*
>    *Protect me in all my endeavors.*
>    *So Mote It Be."*

>*"Spirits of the East,*
>    *Powers of air,*
>    *Come and be present in my circle.*

*Bless me with your clarity, and your
  vision.
Protect me in all my endeavors.
So Mote It Be."*

*"Spirits of the South,
  Powers of fire,
  Come and be present in my circle.
  Bless me with your courage, and your
    passion.
  Protect me in all my endeavors.
  So Mote It Be!"*

*"Spirits of the West,
  Powers of water,
  Come and be present in my circle.
  Bless me with love, and dreams.
  Protect me in all my endeavors.
  So Mote It Be!"*

Stand at the altar.

*"The circle is cast, and we are between the worlds,
beyond the boundaries of time, where night and
day, birth and death, joy and sorrow meet as
one."*

### III. The Body of the Ritual

Here, you celebrate your Sabbat rite, your Esbat, and/or work your magic. Any of the simple rites or spells beginning on page 133 can be performed at this point, or any other ceremonies or magical endeavors you desire.

### IV. Raising and Releasing the Energy

Dance and drum your circle of energy, then release it to the universe. If you are performing a Sabbat ritual, or are not working any particular magic, you can simply dance for the fun of it, or raise and ground the energy purely for the benefit of Mother Earth.

### V. Opening the Circle

Cakes and Ale.

> *"God of the Harvest, bless these cakes,*
> *that we may never hunger.*
> *Goddess of Abundance, bless this drink,*
> *that we may never thirst."*

Thank the spirits of the directions, and bid them farewell.

> *"Spirits of earth (air, water, fire)*
> *I thank you for your blessings.*
> *Return now to your magical realm,*

*With my love and gratitude, that we*
*might meet again*
*Within this sacred circle."*

Thank the God and Goddess, and bid them farewell.

*"Lord and Lady of Magic,*
*I thank you for your blessings.*
*Return now to your magical realm,*
*With my love and gratitude, that we*
*might meet again*
*Within this sacred circle."*

Extinguish the God and Goddess candles.

Open the circle using your wand, athame, or your right hand.

*"I part this circle, all is done*
*Magic forged by Moon and Sun*
*All who came here, thanks to thee*
*To go in peace, and Blessed Be!"*

*"The circle is open, but never broken.*
*Merry meet and merry part, and merry*
*meet again!"*

This ritual is for cleansing and charging your ritual tools, jewelry, or any other sacred objects used in your magic. As discussed earlier, your tools should be consecrated before you use them; this need only be done once. This rite can be combined with the Simple Rite of Dedication on the next page, done on its own, or done any time you add a new treasure to your collection.

**Supplies:**

> Your ritual tools or any other objects that need charging
>
> The four symbolic elements used in consecrating your altar—incense, a red candle, a bowl of water, and a dish of salt

## The Body of the Ritual

Pass the tool through the smoke of the incense.

> *"Inspired with air."*

Pass the tool (quickly!) through the flame of the candle.

> *"Enlightened with fire."*

Sprinkle the tool with water.

> *"Cleansed with water."*

Sprinkle the tool, or simply touch it to the salt.

> *"Strengthened with earth."*

Hold the tool up in salute; picture the energy of the heavens permeating it with light.

> *"Infused with Spirit."*

Set the tool down on the altar, and hold your hands over it in blessing.

> *"By art made, by art changed."*

> *"This wand (athame, pentacle, etc.) shall serve me in this world, between the worlds, and in all the worlds. In the name of the Goddess and of the God, I hereby consecrate this wand. So Mote It Be!"*

## A SIMPLE RITE OF DEDICATION

This ritual is a ceremony of self-dedication in which you pledge yourself to the Craft and the path of the Goddess. Unlike the more formal rites of initiation practiced by many covens, this ceremony is a personal act of commitment, the claiming of your spiritual path in ritual space.

This is a life-changing experience, and one to undertake with deliberation and intent. You can choose to do this at the beginning of your journey, or after you have already studied and practiced the Craft for a time. The Rite of Dedication can be combined with the Simple Rite of Consecration, or done on its own. A great time to do this ritual is at Imbolc, the Sabbat that is symbolic of cleansing and new birth.

In this ritual, you will be reading a personal prayer to the Goddess and God, defining what you desire to manifest in your life as a result of your dedication. A sample of this personal prayer can be found on page 137. You will also be crafting a charm bag containing various objects and elements symbolic to your new life path.

**Supplies:**

One "significator" candle (representative of you), chosen for appropriate color. Good choices would be white for purity, blue for spiritual growth, or purple for spiritual power. Or simply choose your favorite color. (If you do that, you'll likely find the color's meaning is something amazingly magical for you!)

Candleholder

Corresponding magical oil (you might choose ginger for magical power, lavender for purification, or sandalwood for spirituality).

A "magical scroll" (consecrated parchment and ink) containing your personal prayer to the God and Goddess.

Your Cauldron

One small square of cloth or leather

One small stone (earth), one small feather (air), one copper penny (fire), and one small seashell (water) to represent the four elements

Herbs of protection, purification, or spiritual symbolism, if desired

Length of red cord to tie the cloth into a charm bag

### The Body of the Ritual

Dress your significator candle by applying the magical oil from tip to base.

> *"I hereby consecrate this candle in the name of the Goddess, and of the God, that its flame may burn as brightly as the eyes of heaven."*

Light your candle from the flame of the Goddess candle, and set it in its holder.

Read your personal prayer. Roll it up into a scroll, and seal the edges by tipping a few drops of wax from your significator candle onto the paper. Set the scroll on the pentacle at the center of your altar.

*"Tonight by my own free will, and for the highest good of all, I dedicate myself to the Craft of the Wise. I swear to follow this path for only positive means, and to harm none in the process. With pride and reverence, with faith and desire, I call myself Witch. Blessed be this time that marks my life, that I shall ever be a child of the gods, that I shall walk with them, and hold them forever as my own. I swear this in the name of the Goddess, and of the God, and all who preside here within this sacred circle. So Mote It Be!"*

At this point you may wish to perform the Simple Rite of Consecration (page 133) to purify and charge your ritual tools.

Raise and release the energy; when you are finished, touch your prayer scroll to the flame of your significator candle, and let it burn in the cauldron. When the ashes have cooled, tip them onto the center of the cloth square. Add the stone, feather, penny, and seashell; a pinch or two of the sacred herbs; and a few drops of wax from both the Goddess and the God candles. Bring the four corners of the cloth together and bind the bag tightly closed with the red cord.

Finish your ritual. Afterward, place the charm bag on your permanent altar or carry it with you for good fortune and protection.

O Gracious Goddess, O Gracious God, I come to you tonight, freely, with the eyes and the heart of a child, that I may be reborn of your light and your spirit when I leave this sacred circle.

I seek to walk with you, from this moment, in every moment. I ask that you help me continue to grow, and learn, and evolve as a spiritual human, always in your care; to live consciously, in peace and trust, without fear.

Help me to deepen my connection to you and to all that is sacred; to the Earth and her rhythms, the Moon and her cycles, and to all the things that share this collective space.

Help me to make choices in my life, rather than having reactions. Help me learn to allow, to flow with life, and to walk in grace. Help me to integrate and balance my energies, both the dark and the light. Help me to achieve and maintain an optimum level of health in my body, my heart, my mind, and my spirit.

Help me to find a truer, calmer pace, both in my words and in my actions, to create my future with integrity, and to find peace and contentment in the present. Help me to find and recognize more reasons to be happy, to experience more humor, to laugh and play more, and to focus less on challenge or negativity.

Help me learn to love others with more honesty, more compassion, and less judgment; with better personal boundaries; and with far more sanity.

Help me to experience more clarity, insight, and vision, and to manifest what I need and desire from that calm and centered place.

Help me to be patient in all things.

Help me to help others find their true connection to Spirit and to themselves.

Help me to know myself exquisitely, to trust myself implicitly, to honor and care for myself as I would a precious gift. Help me to acknowledge and love the person that I am at any given moment, and above all, help me to be an ordinary woman who does extraordinary things with her life, her love, and her spirit.

O Gracious Goddess, O Gracious God, I ask these things in your presence and in your name, that they may come to me gently and in joy, that they be my truth from this moment on.

So Mote It Be!

## A SIMPLE FULL MOON RITE

In this ritual, you will "Draw Down the Moon," a process of infusing oneself with the energy and life-force of the full moon. You will also read "The Charge of the Goddess," an ancient scripture gifted from the Goddess herself. It is considered an authentic piece of Craft history, handed down in varied versions, from Charles Leland's *Gospel of Aradia,* to Doreen Valiente, and Starhawk's *Spiral Dance.* Beautiful, evocative, magical in itself, the Charge is an essential part of any Esbat ritual.

**Supplies:**

One white pillar candle, in the center of the altar

A copy of the "Charge of the Goddess" (page 143), to be read out loud

Small pieces of parchment paper, upon which you've written anything that you wish to see manifest over the next four weeks

Your cauldron, for burning the pieces of parchment

A Tarot deck, runes, or any other divinatory tool

White and silver are symbolic for this ritual. Try an altar cloth
in white damask, with a quartz crystal ball in the center as a
symbol of the Moon. Silver candlesticks with dangling cut-glass
"crystals" hold the God and Goddess candles; arrange a slender
glass vase with baby's breath and three white roses, and set the
white pillar candle on a round bevel-edged mirror. A huge white
moonsnail shell stands for the Goddess, and a creamy deer
antler represents the God; a few more strategically placed pieces
of clear quartz catch the candlelight, and silver star-shaped confetti is sprinkled everywhere. Breathtaking!

**The Body of the Ritual**

Light the white pillar candle.

Stand at the altar.

> *"Tonight, we welcome the Mother.*
> *Full, and bright in all her glory.*
> *Rich, milk-white Goddess of mystery*
> *  and light*
> *Come, blessed Moon,*
> *Lady of Magic."*

> *"Pour your light over me.*
> *Fill me with your fire.*
> *Blood and bone, bright with your power,*
> *Witch and Goddess are one."*

Draw Down the Moon.

Take your athame in your right hand. Take a deep breath and center yourself. Raise your arms above you, as if welcoming heaven. If you are outside, *be* in the moonlight. If you are indoors, *imagine*.

The Goddess silvers the sky and all the Earth below her. Her light is cool, translucent, streaming down in glittering waves and washing over everything, over you. Breathe it in. Close your eyes and open your crown chakra, on the top of your head, and your heart center, just above your solar plexus; let the moonlight flood inside of you. Breathe more deeply, as the energy animates you. Your body quickens; your skin feels electrified as you take in more and more of the Goddess' power. You open your eyes, and they burn in the darkness; the eyes of a wolf, a tiger, a creature of instinct in the deepest forest at midnight. Everything is sharp, focused, charged with light; you *are* the Goddess embodied, and magic is indeed afoot!

Read the "Charge of the Goddess."

Perform any other spellwork, consecration of tools, etc.

Give thanks for wish fulfillment, or something else that has occurred since the last Moon Rite.

Read your new wish aloud. (If in a group setting and privacy is an issue, read your wish silently.) Light the parchment with the flame of the pillar candle, and drop it into the cauldron.

> *"Goddess Silver, Goddess Bright*
> *Take this wish from me tonight.*
> *Full, to dark, and round again,*
> *Please grant this wish for me by then."*

Choose a rune or Tarot card and interpret it as a message from the Goddess regarding the coming four weeks.

## THE CHARGE OF THE GODDESS

Hear my words, and know me. I shall be called by many names, in many tongues; past ancient days, beyond this moment, and through the end of time—at once Artemis, Diana, Ishtar, Aphrodite, Venus, the Morrigan, and Queen of the Witches. I am the Great Goddess, Mother of All.

Whenever you have need of my aid—once a month and best when the Moon is full—shall you assemble in some secret place, to call me and to honor my spirit. Know that my truths and my love shall make you free, for no man can enslave you, or prevent your worship of me in your mind and in your heart. I require no sacrifice or pain of your bodies, for I am the Mother of all living things, and my only law is Love Unto All.

Listen well when you come into my presence, and I shall teach you of deep mysteries, ancient and powerful, the rhythms of the planets and the seasons, the circle of life and death and life renewed. That which is unknown shall be known, and that which is hidden shall be revealed; even the most secretive soul shall find illumination in me.

For I am the beauty of the green Earth, the silver Moon that sails among the stars, the mystery of the flowing waters, and the desire of the heart of Man. From me all things are born, and to me all things in their season return. Let my joyous worship be in your hearts; dance, sing, and feast in my name, for all acts of love and pleasure are my rituals. Let there be beauty and strength, power and compassion, honor and humility, mirth and reverence within you, for these are the gifts I offer to all my children.

And you who seek to know me, know that your seeking and yearning will avail you not, unless you know the Mystery—for if that which you seek you find not within yourself, you will never find it without.

Hear my words, and know me truly; Lady of Moonlight and Magic; Maiden, Mother, and Crone. For behold, I have been with you from the beginning, and I will welcome you into my arms once more at the end of all your days.

## A SIMPLE CANDLE SPELL

This spell can be used for both attraction and banishing.

**Supplies:**

One candle, chosen for appropriate color

Corresponding magical oil

Candleholder

Your magical scroll, with your statement of intent written upon it

Visual aids such as photos, drawings, or Tarot cards, placed upon the altar

### The Body of the Ritual

If desired, carve runes, symbols, or appropriate words into the candle with your bolline. Dress the candle by applying the oil from tip to base for attraction magic, from base to tip for banishing.

> *"I hereby consecrate this candle in the name of the*
> *Goddess, and of the God, that its flame may burn*
> *as brightly as the eyes of heaven."*

Place the candle in its holder, and light it.

> *"Blessed candle, sacred flame*
> *Burning in the Goddess' name [or call a*
> *specific deity, such as Brigid or Astarte]*
> *Hear my prayer and know my need*
> *Grant my wish with magic speed."*

Read your statement of intent. Roll it up into a scroll, and seal the edge by tipping a few drops of the candlewax onto the paper. Set the scroll on your altar pentacle, and let the candle burn out as you raise and release the energy.

> *"In no way will this spell reverse, or place upon*
> *me any curse. In the name of the Goddess, and of*
> *the God, I proclaim this spell complete. So Mote*
> *It Be!"*

When you are finished with your ritual, warm any wax left over from the candle and affix it to the seal or tuck it inside the scroll. Place the scroll on your permanent altar, or someplace safe, until your spell comes to fruition. Then burn the paper in your cauldron as a thank you to the Goddess.

This spell is one of my favorites for manifesting, or bringing something into your life. This can be used in conjunction with the Simple Candle Spell; it's fun, and packs quite a magical punch.

**Supplies:**

Your magical scroll, with your statement of intent written upon it

A length of red cord

## The Body of the Ritual

Read your statement of intent. Spend some time visualizing the result, and focus your energy into the scroll. Roll up the scroll and wrap it with the red cord, tying nine knots in accordance with the following rhyme:

*"By knot of one, the spell's begun.* (Tie the first knot.)

*By knot of two, it cometh true.* (Tie the second knot, and so on.)

*By knot of three, So Mote It Be.*

*By knot of four, tis 'strengthened more.*

*By knot of five, this spell's alive.*

*By knot of six, this spell I fix.*

*By knot of seven, the Powers in Heaven.*
*By knot of eight, 'tis sealed with fate.*
*By knot of nine, this spell's divine.*
*By the Goddess' hand, this thing is mine!"*

Set the scroll on your altar pentacle, and raise and release the energy.

*"In no way will this spell reverse, or place upon*
*me any curse. In the name of the Goddess, and of*
*the God, I proclaim this spell complete. So Mote*
*It Be!"*

Afterward, keep the scroll somewhere safe until the spell comes to fruition. Then burn the scroll in your cauldron as a thank you to the Goddess.

# eleven

# FULL CIRCLE

*Honor the Old Ones in deed and name,*
*let love and light be our guides again.*

—The Wiccan Rede

Early morning, late October. The world is still dark; the head-lamps of cars gleam on the wet pavement beyond the gate; a few last stars huddle in the damp clouds that mute the sky. I hunch down into jacket and garden boots, dragging the garbage cans to the curb through the muddy grass; *way* too soon to be up, after way too little sleep, after way too close a call making my daughter's school bus, after cats knocking over plants in the living room *yet again*, after running out of milk before breakfast ... what? Me, crabby? My life *ordinary?* Hah!

I set the cans in their proper places, ten feet from streetside, handles facing *out;* I turn to go back to the house, wondering if a certain pair of kittens would clog up the vacuum hose if I dare indulge a momentary fantasy. And there She is, smiling down at me and my mutterings, a scarf of mist veiling Her face through the suddenly shattered clouds.

I don't know for how long I stood there, gazing. I do know that in an instant I was transformed. In a trail of moonlight I went back inside, and the carpet got swept, and the cats wound themselves, charmingly, around my feet. The sky lightened, and the day unfolded in all its beautiful and mundane glory; I thought about the Goddess, and the God, through grocery lines and seventh-grade homework and soup for dinner, and through all the moments that passed. And that night, after tucking in kid and critters, I saw Her again, my celestial guardian; shining silver through my bedroom window as I turned out the lights and wound my way down into sleep.

Wicca is not just a path to follow, it is a life to live, a life of awareness, hope, and love. A Witch's eyes are open in ways that others' are not; we see Divinity in the shapes of leaves, in the patterns of the stars, in the colors of an autumn field, and in the ladybug sunning itself on the mailbox on a February afternoon. Our ears are tuned to music in things like water over stones, and crickets in the sunflowers, and simple words that can be chanted aloud in the moonlight. We take responsibility for our words and actions—for ourselves, our planet, and our fellow beings, knowing that what goes around, comes around, and then some, and we create our lives accordingly. And our hearts are open to Spirit in ways that I can find no words or images to describe.

Living Wicca is living *connected,* to Heaven, the Earth, and everything in between. To truly live the path of Wicca is to get involved; not just performing rituals and spells but spreading magic throughout your life and community. Recycle. Use Earth-friendly organic products and support local merchants who do the same. Join neighborhood cleanup projects, or initiate your own. Support groups and organizations that help the environment, animals, and humans in need. Write "letters to the editor" and to Congress to support these same causes and to oppose destructive policies and practices. Educate others, either locally or globally, about the *truth* of the Craft, and help wipe out the lies and misconceptions once and for all.

Practice compassion. Realize that everyone is doing the best they can, at any given moment, including yourself. Take time for kindness. Seek the conscious, and peaceful, alternative. Find something good in everyone and everything. And every day, seek magic in the simple moments.

Notice Spirit everywhere. It's easy in nature—take a walk in the park and watch the trees change, sit on a rock by the river and listen to the voice of the Earth, stand on the beach at sunset and count the waves between you and the Moon. In the settings of the modern world, it gets a little harder. But for the sake of our planet and our people, this is where it really counts.

Spells can be woven outside of the sacred circle as well. Watch for Wiccan bumper stickers on the cars around you in rush-hour traffic. Some of my favorites are "The Goddess Is Alive, And Magic Is Afoot," "My Other Car Is A Broom," and

"Back Off, I'm A Goddess." Salute your common connection with a wave or a smile. Send blessings—rather than cursings—to all the other frustrated drivers out there (remember well the Threefold Law!). You might be surprised at how quickly you make it to your destination!

Check out the "altar" a coworker has constructed on their desk—a favorite photo grouped with a plant and a feather found on a lunch break. Comment on it, and venture to ask if it was instinctual, or intended. You might find a fellow Wiccan in your midst! If not, you've just raised the spiritual temperature of your workplace, simply by acknowledgment.

When you're cleaning house, you can visualize universal energy pouring through your dust rag, mop, and vacuum, eliminating every bit of dirt and negativity. Chant a little ditty such as "Shadows gone, Light be seen; This room now sacred, blessed, and clean."

You can even turn housework into a great little banishing ritual for yourself as well: Write whatever you would like to see removed from your life, such as debt, frustration, or illness, on a piece of magically charged paper. Then tear the paper up in little pieces (this feels good just by itself!), throw them on the floor, and vacuum, picturing the issue being sucked up into the void with the scraps. You can also write on the mirror or the counter in lipstick or grease pencil, or on the bathroom tile with colored soap, then wipe away your troubles.

Food is another great spiritual catalyst. The simplest thing, of course, is giving thanks to the God and Goddess for their bounty before each meal. Picture the power of the gods infusing your food before you eat, infusing *you* with health and happiness. Prepare recipes with magically charged ingredients, and every once in awhile, eat by candlelight in the middle of the sacred circle.

Set up a permanent altar in your home and spend some time there morning and night in prayer and meditation. It only takes a moment to connect with Spirit, and it will help keep you connected all day. Have an offering bowl, and leave pennies, beads, herbs, stones, or things you might find as you go about your daily routine as a thank you for your many blessings.

Smile at strangers. Say hello to the person standing next to you in line at the post office. Tell someone that you like the color of their sweater, or that their baby is probably the cutest thing you've ever seen. Picture people surrounded by their own magic circle of light, health, and happiness. Spend time with the people you love and, most important, speak your love. No one can ever hear "I love you," spoken in truth and from the soul, enough.

The God and Goddess are everywhere, in everyone, and in everything. Remember this. Live your life from that knowing place, and you will hold the space for others to do so, and be blessed beyond imagining.

# TO LEARN MORE

There are many wonderful books available to guide you on the Wiccan path. Following are just a few:

*The Beltane Papers: A Journal of Women's Mysteries*. Bellingham, WA. The Brideswell Collective. *Sage Woman*. Point Arena, CA: Blessed Bee, Inc. These are quarterly publications with wonderful seasonal art, poetry, stories, and celebrations. Great ads in the back for Pagan catalogs and other sources. Subscriptions available.

Cabot, Laurie. *Power of the Witch*. New York: Delta Publications, 1989. Powerful, strong text; *intense* historical narrative; a focus on the "science" of Witchcraft—states of consciousness, psychic diagnosis of disease, etc.; also a great Table of Correspondences.

Campanelli, Pauline. *Wheel of the Year: Living the Magical Life*. St. Paul, MN: Llewellyn Publications, 1989. A wonderful book that not only celebrates the Sabbats, but gives you myriad ways to live magically all year—food, crafts, Earthlore, and symbology.

Conway, D. J. *Moon Magic*. St. Paul, MN: Llewellyn Publications, 1995. Legends, deities, food, drink, and fascinations dedicated entirely to the Goddess Moon—an indispensable resource for Esbat ritual.

Cunningham, Scott. *Wicca: A Guide for the Solitary Practitioner*. St. Paul, MN: Llewellyn Publications, 1988. Gentle, simple rituals and a solid communication of the intricacies of Wicca, without sacrificing the magic.

K., Amber. *Covencraft: Witchcraft for Three or More*. St. Paul, MN: Llewellyn Publications, 1998. The definitive work on covens and group ritual.

*Llewellyn's Magical Almanac*. St. Paul, MN: Llewellyn Publications. Published yearly, this book contains a magical calendar, spells, rituals, recipes, and stories from all the Who's Who of Wiccan and Pagan writers.

McCoy, Edain. *The Sabbats*. St. Paul, MN: Llewellyn Publications, 1994. An essential compilation of holiday lore, tradition, and observances; rituals for both group and solitary practice; and wonderful recipes! Great at-a-glance Sabbat Tables of Correspondences.

Medbh-Mara, Aeron. *Life Rites*. Leicestershire, 1995. Thoth Publications. This little book holds some of the most lyrical rituals ever composed. Rites of handfasting, birth, adopting, the ending of relationship; rituals for new mothers, new fathers, coming of age for male and female, and beautiful rituals for death and requiem. Clear and concise information regarding ministry, coven work, and performing rites for others.

Renee, Janina. *Tarot Spells.* St. Paul, MN: Llewellyn Publications, 1990. Great spells in this book! The simple and fun rituals use the Tarot as a specific magical catalyst.

Silver RavenWolf. *To Ride a Silver Broomstick: New Generation Witchcraft.* St. Paul, MN: Llewellyn Publications, 1993. Great fun, quick wit, and a ton of information! Excellent chapters on ritual supplies and color magic, and an extensive listing of Pagan newsletters and services.

Stein, Diane. *A Women's Book of Ritual.* Freedom, CA: The Crossing Press, 1990. A marvelous book filled with powerful Goddess rituals that heal and inspire.

Telesco, Patricia. *A Victorian Grimoire.* St. Paul, MN: Llewellyn Publications, 1992. Kitchen magic, herbs, spells for the home, the kids, the critters; the Wheel of the Year and the Moon all done up with Victorian history and flair.

Weinstein, Marion. *Positive Magic.* Custer, WA: Phoenix Publishing Inc., 1981. A classic. Don't be without this book.

*The Witches' Almanac.* Middletown, RI: Published in cooperation with Capra Press, Santa Barbara. This volume is released each spring; full of magical lore, little rituals, astrological forecasts, and a great calendar with the phases of the Moon and the planets.

# WEBSITES FOR
# THE WICCAN COMMUNITY

**BlessedBe.com**

www.BlessedBe.com

Promoting understanding and tolerance of witchcraft through education. This site addresses Wicca and Witchcraft from an intellectual perspective, providing sources and definitions in order to provide accurate historical information to browsers.

**The Witches' Web**

www.witchesweb.com

A Pagan news, education, and networking site. The most popular feature of this site is The Witches' Web of Days, an online book of days of birthdays, celebrations and observances.

**Black-Raven**

www.black-raven.com

Information on Wicca, the Elements, Stones, Spells, Deities, Astrology, Herbs, and Magick.

**www.Wicca.com**

This is one of the largest Wicca, Pagan, and Witchcraft sites on the web. Includes message areas, online chat rooms, and a catalog of magikal products.

### Celtic Connection

www.celticconnection.com

Wiccan, witchcraft, and Pagan knowledge and supplies are shared and listed throughout the site.

### Witch Vox

www.witchvox.com

Offers daily updates news related to the Modern Pagan Community. Features 30,000 links and contacts for networking.

### The Witches' League for Public Awareness

www.CelticCrow.com

This site stresses the need for public awareness of Wiccans in the news and other media, and offers witchcraft basics and community resources.

### Covent of the Goddess (CoGWeb)

www.cog.org

This is the homepage of the Covent of the Goddess, an international organization of cooperating, autonomous Wiccan congregations and solitary practitioners.

# ACKNOWLEDGMENTS

This book represents the powerful combination of a long sought-after goal, a dream realized, and a definitive coming of age.

I wish to thank the following people, who helped to make it possible:

Mary Jane Ryan, my editor, for her integrity, her willingness to listen and, even more so, to *hear;* for her no-nonsense style laced with sensitivity and laughter. I could not have asked for a better guide on this, my maiden voyage.

Carol Roth, for affording me this opportunity, and for bringing us full circle.

Rev. Judith Laxer—Judishka, my favorite Witch—for her insights, her friendship, and that amazing laugh.

Catherine Ponder, whose inspirational guidance brought me here, and continues to lead me into my "promised land."

Kim Schneider—a Goddess in her own right, who has talked me down from every ledge, helped me to see myself through Spirit's eyes, and is, and always will be, the truest friend I could ever have. I will never find the words to express what our friendship means to me, but I will keep searching ... in the meantime (and for all time), I love you.

David Swain, my photographer, for capturing the Moon, and sharing a history.

Nan Yurkanis, for truly being a "warrior in my tribe." Shine on, little sister!

My family—Mom, Dad, Mitch, April, Chelsea, and Shayne, for loving and supporting me, always.

And my daughter, Kaeleigh. For giving up "Mom time" in the evenings without complaint and for hanging out with me in my office so I could glue myself to the computer keyboard with company; for nights of "Practical Magic," and sleepovers, and kittens, and M&Ms; and, most of all, for choosing to come into this world through me. You are an extraordinary young woman, and I love you madly.

I would also like to acknowledge the following as masters, and definitely as my teachers: Brigid Rowan, Rev. Judith Laxer, Tess Sterling, Scott Cunningham, Silver RavenWolf, D. J. Conway, Diane Stein, Laurie Cabot, Catherine Ponder, Edain McCoy, Pauline Campanelli, Patricia Telesco, Starhawk, and Marion Weinstein. Your teachings have blessed my life in untold ways, allowed me to work countless miracles, and afforded me a spiritual expression that completely fulfills and sustains me. And your words, married with mine, helped to inspire the whole of this work and to create the rituals in chapter 10, especially.

Thank you . . . heart and soul.

And to all those who read this book—brightest blessings to every one of you, and may the God and Goddess walk with you always.

# INDEX

## ABOUT THE AUTHOR

Michele Morgan has been dedicated to the path of Wicca, mainly as a solitary practitioner, for the past seven years. She incorporates many aspects of Wicca into her work as a professional psychic, Tarot counselor, certified NLP Practitioner, writer, and teacher. Her private practice is based in Seattle, Washington, and she also holds a staff position as an intuitive consultant at EastWest Bookshop, one of the largest metaphysical bookstores in the Northwest. In addition to a Tarot advice column and monthly psychic insights on her popular Web site, Morgan wrote the script and consulted on Sting's 1995 CD-ROM project, "All This Time." She lives in a magical house in Snohomish, Washington, with her daughter, their dog, and three cats. You can contact her at her Web site at www.heartoftheraven.com.